Old Stone Crosses
of
West
Gloucestershire

By
Ruth Proctor Hirst

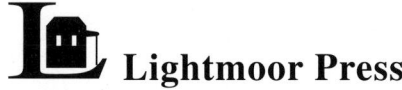

Lightmoor Press

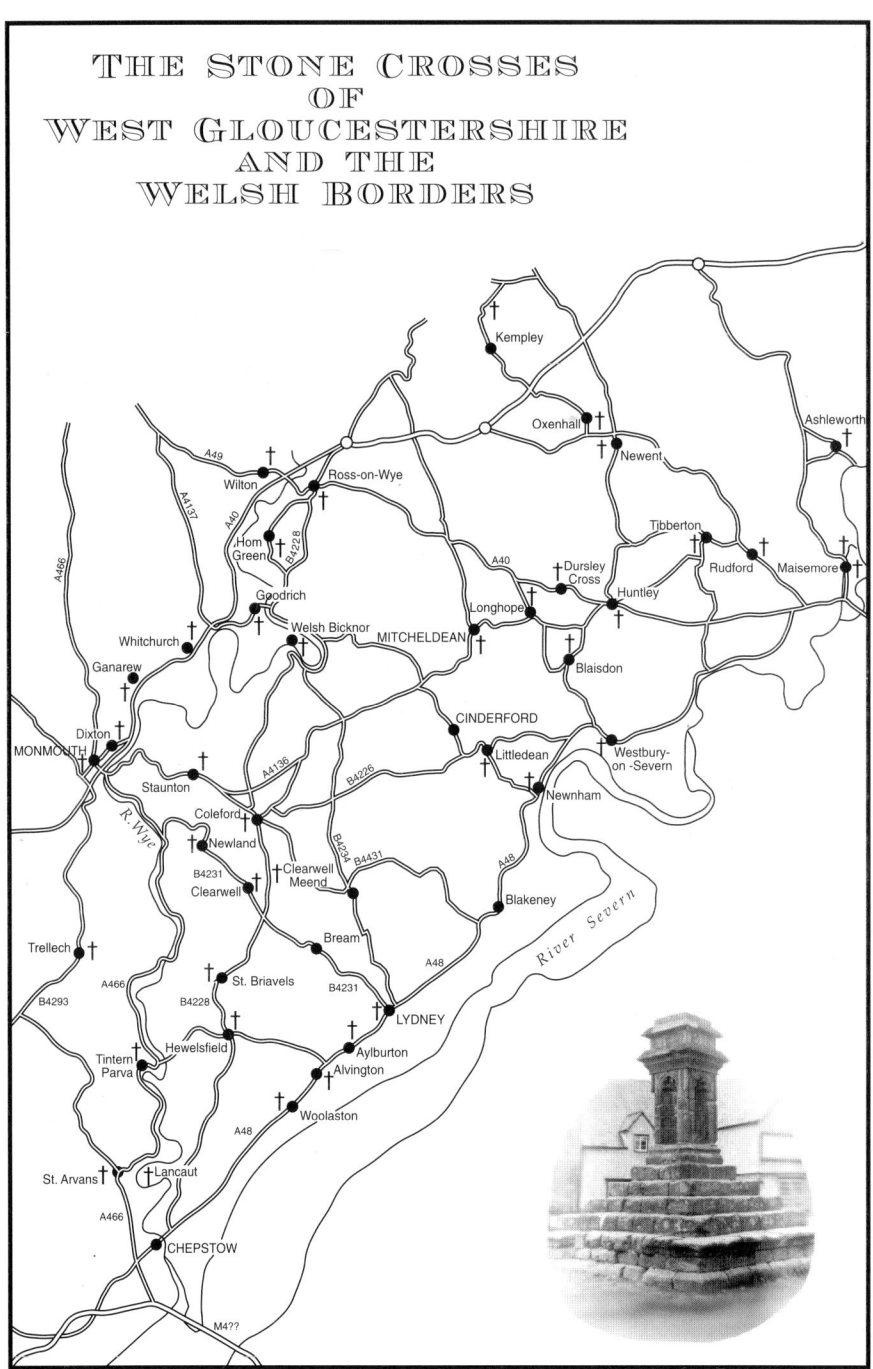

INTRODUCTION

ALTHOUGH from my earliest days I was aware of those beauties of architectural style at Lydney, Aylburton and Clearwell, I first became seriously interested in the ancient stone crosses whilst living in Cornwall (1950-85), where there are over 600 of various types and state of preservation – and where, even now, 'new' ones are quite often being discovered. Having studied the Cornish monuments, on my return to the Forest of Dean, I decided to learn more about the crosses in the different counties of England, (and I use the old names), with special attention on those of Gloucestershire and more particularly still, those between Severn and Wye; although I have also searched for any in the neighbouring counties of Monmouth and Herefordshire with some success. It is not only those monuments still extant that are of interest; indeed, the sites of the lost crosses are most significant (i.e. the High Cross, Newnham). Some War Memorials have been placed on an ancient site, some even incorporating part of the old monument. Two to the north of the area, both on the west side of the Severn, which stand in the 'right' position are the memorials in Chaceley and Tirley churchyards; can either or both have been the site of a churchyard cross? Though most of the crosses are in churchyards, usually on the south side of the church – as some would have it, 'so that the shadow of the building did not fall on it' – others are by the roadside; often placed as boundary markers to ecclesiastic or other estates. Many have been restored to commemorate some special event, such as Westbury on Severn's village cross restored for Queen Victoria's Jubilee in 1887; while Ross's Plague Cross in the churchyard is self-explanatory.

The Bounds of the Forest

The Bounds of the Forest of Dean of 1282 included two crosses[1] – that of Dunne's Cross (from ford, Goodrich to Mersty Lane), and Luce Cross (millpond Buriton, Luce Cross and thence by the King's Highway through Gorsley). Unfortunately, to date, the writer has not been able to trace either's probable site. Although the churches at English Bicknor and Ruardean are among the few ancient churches of the Forest of Dean, apparently no cross, churchyard or otherwise, is recorded at either place. However, Ruardean (1111) has two points of interest. The first is the unusually shaped font, fairly rare for being dated (1657) and which was installed during the days of the Commonwealth. The other is the Norman tympanum over the south door. It is one of the rare ones showing Saint George on horseback, slaying the dragon. David Verey (1970)[2] says: 'It is of unusual quality belonging to the Herefordshire School of Sculpture, 1130-60.'

[1] *Regard of the Forest of Dean 1282*. Hart, C. 1987
[2] *Shell Guide – Gloucestershire*. Very, D. 1970

Place Names

Although there are several place names with 'cross' in them, there may be no actual monument there now – or ever have been, simply just a crossroad. Smithers Cross is one place in question, named for the smithy which stood there. Tibbs Cross on the old Dean Road, also had no apparent structure either. The writer has heard no legends of either place, but Deadman's Cross, also on the Dean Road, has at least two to relate. The one is that a headless horseman rides up and down at certain times and local children would be threatened with tales of him to ensure good behaviour. The other came to light during the recent survey of the Road carried out by members of the Forest of Dean Local History Society; in that, two Roman soldiers fought a dual at the crossing, with one being fatally injured and being buried at or near it. Among some of the other cross place names – all apparently only crossroads – there are Drybrook Cross and Parkend Cross. At Staunton (by Gloucester, NGR SO 792294), the crossroads are referred to as the Cross, although there is apparently no record of one having been there; nor could the writer learn of one at the aptly-named Hethelpit Cross further along the A417 road towards Hereford.

In my own village of Bream, although no cross is shown a map of 1608 at the aptly-named Breams Cross – yet another crossroads – two others seem to be marked thus ☩. One appears on what was up to only a few years ago, a grassy triangle opposite the church, and the other was probably somewhere near the present crossroads at the schools.

Sources

In 1868 Charles Pooley published his work on the *Old Crosses of Gloucestershire* and this has been the basis for my research – very much an on-going one. However, there are quite a number he did not cover, i.e. Huntley and Woolaston to name but two. Church guides are usually a useful source, providing the writer found the monument of interest, and I have learnt of missing crosses from them. That at Forthampton is a good example where a chapel and dovecot built 'near the village cross' was converted into two cottages in the 17th century and are now known as 'The Sanctuary' (1975).

Besides guide books and magazine articles, information regarding a cross can often be obtained from a local paper and it was one such which alerted the writer to the fact that Brockweir (NGR SO 541012) once had a cross. 'Cross House', built in 1514, took its name from the cross which stood on the village green until the early 19th century. It was demolished to make way for the building of the New Inn, now the Brockweir Inn.

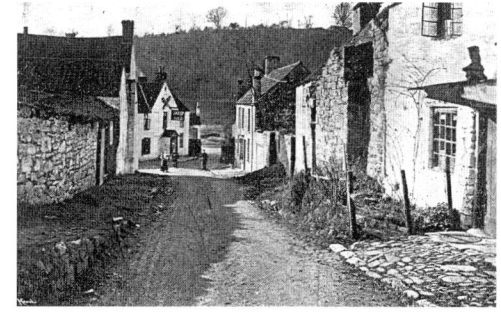

Main Street in Brockweir taken in 1905. The New Inn at the bottom of the street was the site of the cross.

GAZETTEER

O.S. 1: 50,000 Series Maps:
Nos. 149. 150. 162.

Alvington	Gloucestershire	Maisemore	Gloucestershire
Ashleworth	"	*Churchyard*	
Aylburton	"	*Bridge*	
		Mitcheldean	"
Blaisdon	"		
		Newent	"
Clearwell	"	*Church*	
Village	"	*Market Hall*	
Gattle Stone	"	Newland	"
Coleford	"	Newnham on Severn	"
Deerhurst	"	Oxenhall	
Dixton	Monmouthshire		
Churchyard		Ross on Wye	Herefordshire
Museum		*Churchyard*	
Over Monnow		*Edde Cross*	
Dursley Cross	Gloucestershire	*Wilton Ferry Cross*	
		Rudford	Gloucestershire
Ganarew	Herefordshire		
Churchyard		St Arvans	Monmouthshire
Wayside		St Briavels	Gloucestershire
Goodrich	"	Staunton	"
Churchyard			
Goodrich Cross		Tibberton	"
		Tintern Parva	Monmouthshire
Hewelsfield	Gloucestershire	Trellech	"
Hom Green	Herefordshire	*Churchyard*	
Huntley	Gloucestershire	*Trellech Cross*	
Kempley	"	Welsh Bicknor	Herefordshire
		Westbury on Severn	Gloucestershire
Lancaut	"	*Village*	
Littledean	"	*Six Bells*	
Longhope	"	*Chaxhill*	
Churchyard		Whitchurch	Herefordshire
Wayside		Woolaston	Gloucestershire
Lydney	"		

ALVINGTON. Glos.

NGR SO 604006 Sheet 162

In the church, high up in a blocked-up lancet window at the west end of the nave, is preserved a gable cross with an incised Cross on its face. In the churchyard, to the south of the church, is a round grassy mound probably the site of the former churchyard cross which is often to be found at or near this position. The stones of this monument were removed to Clanna Woods to await re-erection when it was dismantled in the early 19th century. It was believed that they were lost but in 1997 they were 'rediscovered' in a private garden.

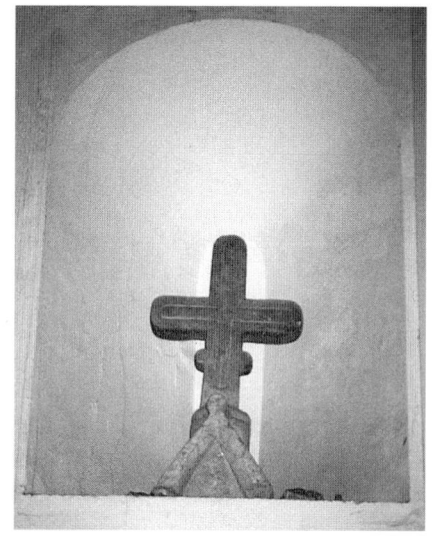

Right. The preserved gable cross.

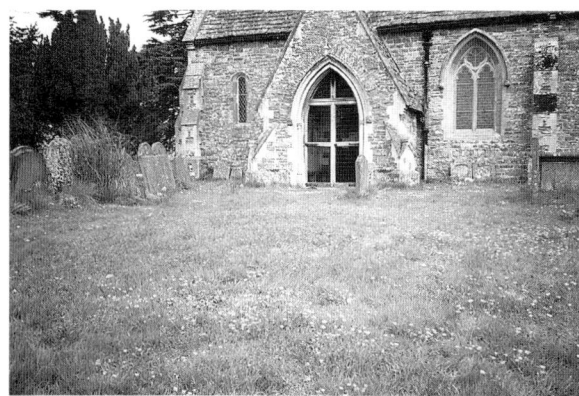

The possible site of Alvington cross is marked by a slight mound in the churchyard. The stones of the cross were removed in the early 19th century.

The base stone from Alvington Cross which now forms part of an ornamental fountain.

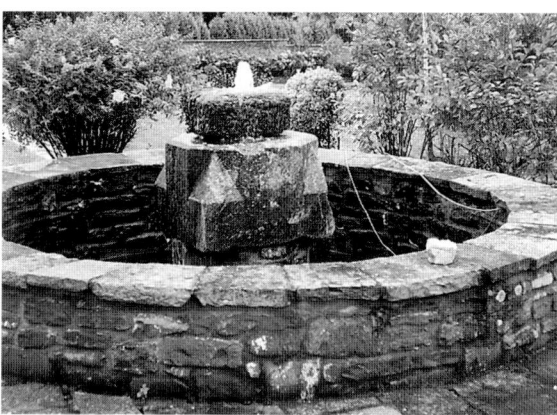

ASHLEWORTH. Glos.

NGR SO 814255 Sheet 162

This restored 14th century cross stands on the Green some distance from the ancient church which is situated nearer the River Severn. It has had a varied life, with different guide books saying it is on the Green, and others that it is in the churchyard. It appears that the head was found in the early 19th century hidden in a chimney stack, having been placed there for safety in Cromwell's time. It was then set up in the churchyard; however, in the early 1970s Mr. F. J. Chamberlayne paid to have it removed and replaced on its original steps on the Green, where it now proudly stands. The canopied head has figures in each of its four niches, one of them showing the Crucifixion, while the reverse side, though somewhat damaged, shows the Virgin and Child with a young woman kneeling at one side. Both side niches have figures but they are rather worn and indistinguishable.

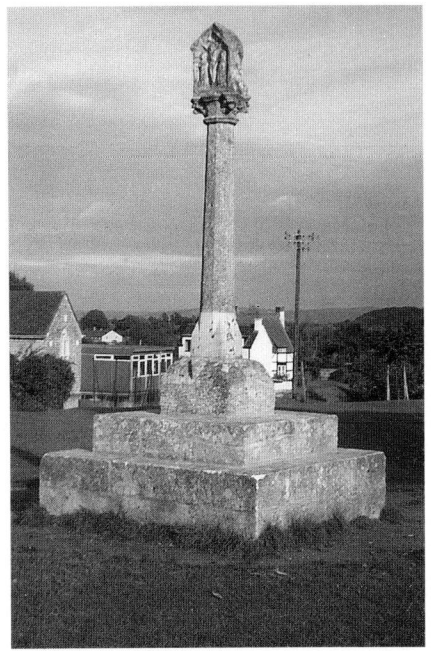

Ashleworth cross as re-erected on the village green in the early 1970s.

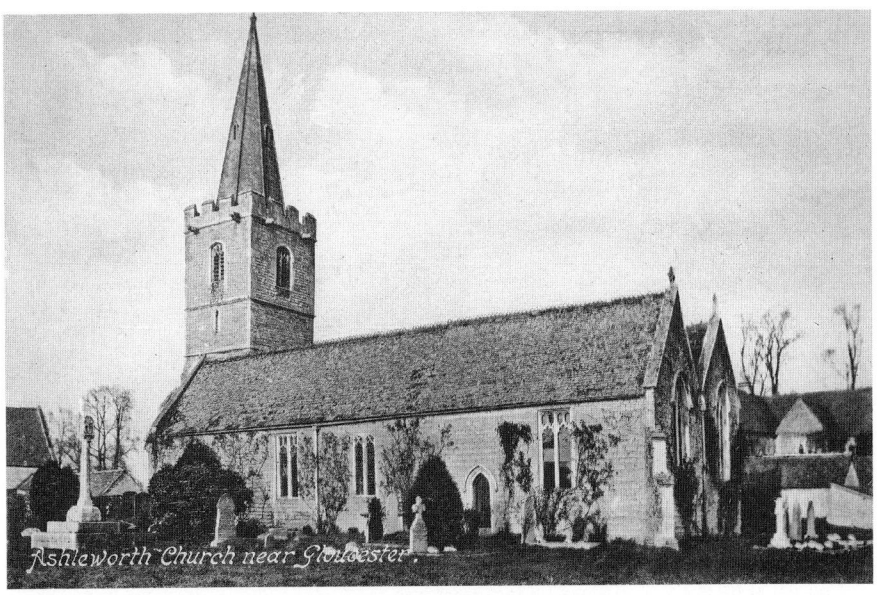

The cross in its original position in the churchyard can be seen on the left of this c1910 view.

AYLBURTON. Glos.
NGR SO 617017 Sheet 162
Ancient Monument.

Used by travelling friars to preach to the people, this cross, of the 14th century, consists of five steps and base with niches for figures, and stands at the side of the A48 road near the 'Cross' Inn. It had been repaired in 1841, and in the early 1960s it was moved back a few yards from its original site as it had become a traffic hazard. In an effort to stop car parking against this ancient monument, a paved area with a seat, plus bollards with chains, was made in 1993. Prior to 1915 when the present Methodist Chapel was built, the first services were held at the cross, later they were held in the old Malt House until the chapel was built. There is a reference to a party of laymen who walked from Whitecroft via Bream over the Common to Aylburton where they stopped at the cross for prayers.

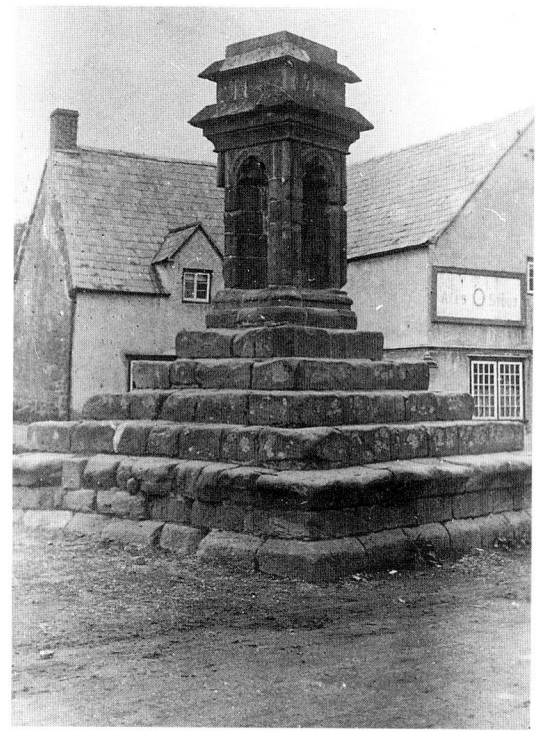

A close up of the cross around the turn of the century.

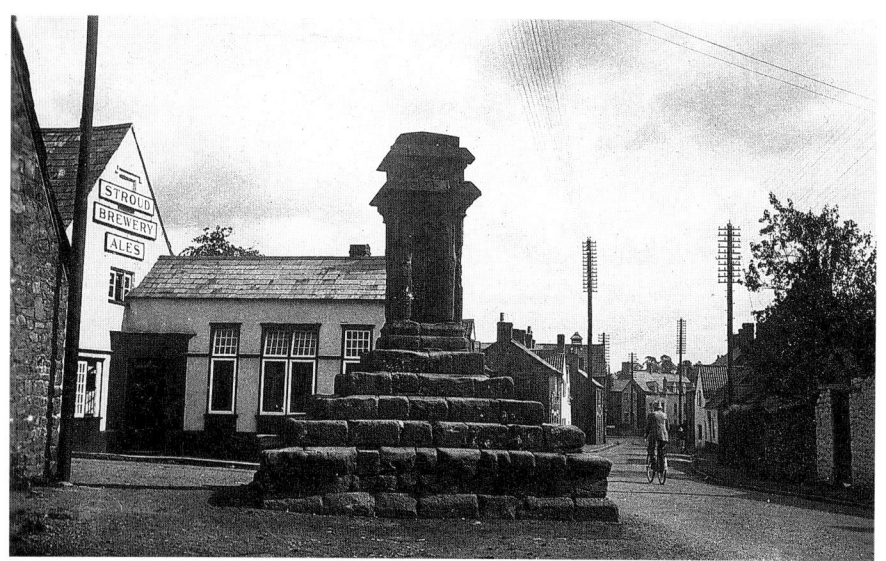

A 1930s postcard scene of the cross, looking along the main road towards Lydney.

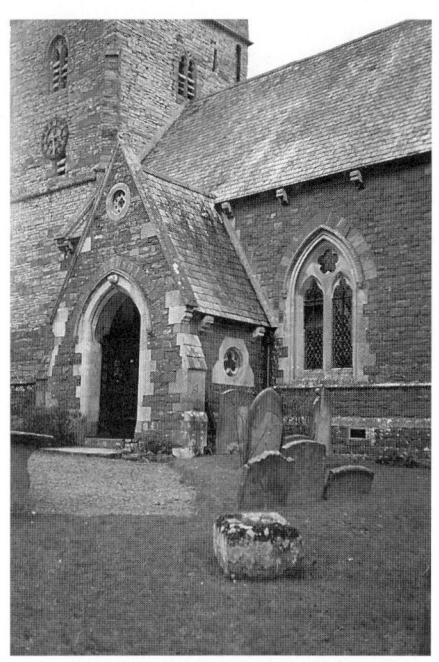

BLAISDON. Glos.

NGR SO 703172 Sheet 162

Only the tower of the medieval church of St Michael remains following the rebuilding of 1867-9. Set on a bank above the road, there is a fine view of the distant Cotswolds from the churchyard. A square stone base with chamfered top, stands to the right of the south door of Blaisdon church. It measures approximately 23ins. square with a 3ins. bevel to approximately 18ins. at the top. The shaft has been cut off level with the top of the stone and measured 8ins. by 7ins.

Left. *The stone base standing in the churchyard.*

Below. *A close up of the base showing where the shaft has been cut off level with the top of the stone.*

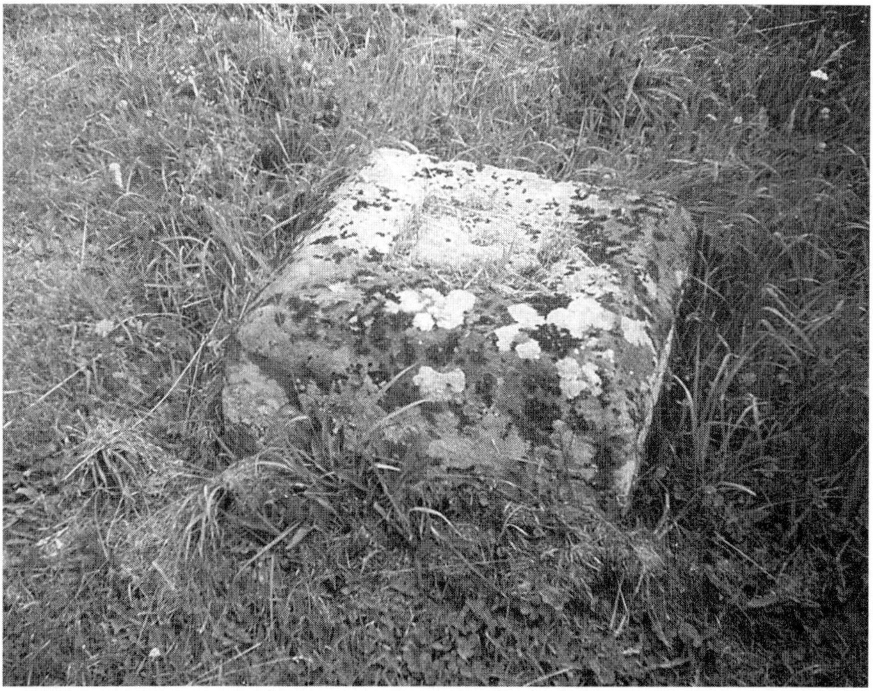

CLEARWELL. Glos.

NGR SO 572081 Sheet 162

Ancient Monument.

This restored 14th century cross stands at the bottom of the street where the road from Coleford meets the B4231. The shrine and five steps on which it stands, are original, but the shaft and head were made new in the restoration of circa 1866. Previous to this (circa 1840), the stump had been topped by a brightly coloured cock, but thanks to Caroline, Countess Dunraven, this was removed and replaced in a more becoming style, designed by John Middleton, probably at the time he built the church (1866). The cross was repaired in 1975, but in 1987 it was noted that the head was missing; later it was learnt that it was being preserved at a nearby house. In 1991 work, carried out by Stonewest Cox of Cheltenham, began on the restoration, total cost of which was £10,000. Because it is a listed monument, half of the cost was met by English Heritage with the villagers contributing to the rest. There are now bollards at each corner for protection. This cross was not shown on either the 1608 map or Taylor's map of 1777. However, one is noted on the earlier map at a site now only recalled by the name of 'Lower Cross.' (*NGR SO 568083 Sheet 162*).

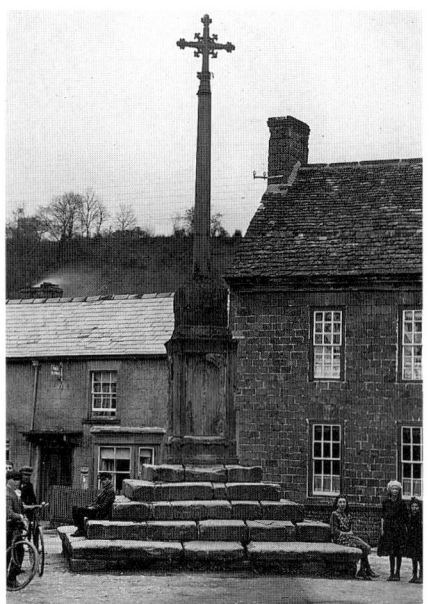

Clearwell Cross seen around 1920.

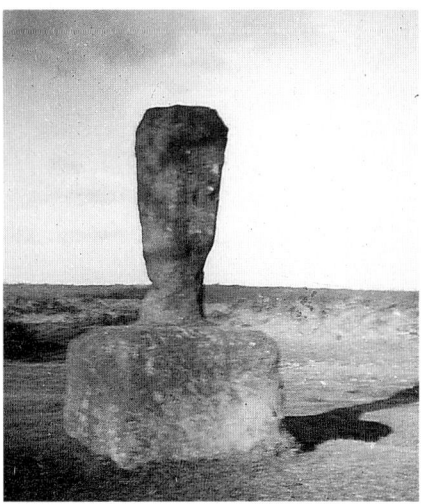

The Gattle stone on Clearwell Meend.

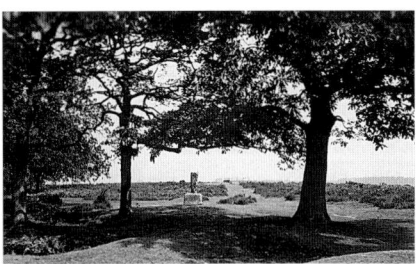

Gattle Stone.

NGR SO 581085 Sheet 162

This monument stands at the side of the B4228, on Clearwell Meend, on a part known as the Scar. Also known as 'Caradoc's Stone', 'Gattle's Cross', and 'Milo's Cross' as well as the 'Blood Stone'

-the latter name derived from the local folklore that if it is pricked with a pin it will bleed. The present structure is of the 18th or 19th century, but most probably replaces an earlier stone said to have been set up as a bound stone in 1282.

COLEFORD. Glos.
Missing.

Coleford, according to a map of 1608 had its preaching cross in the town centre near the Old Chapel, which was probably demolished circa 1679 when the Market Hall was erected, this latter too, was demolished in the 1960s. There is a modern memorial cross erected on the site of the altar of the chapel demolished 1882.

Also shown on this map a CROSSE OF HAND is marked near Edge End, approximately NGR SO 593131, the present road runs at a different level to that of that date.

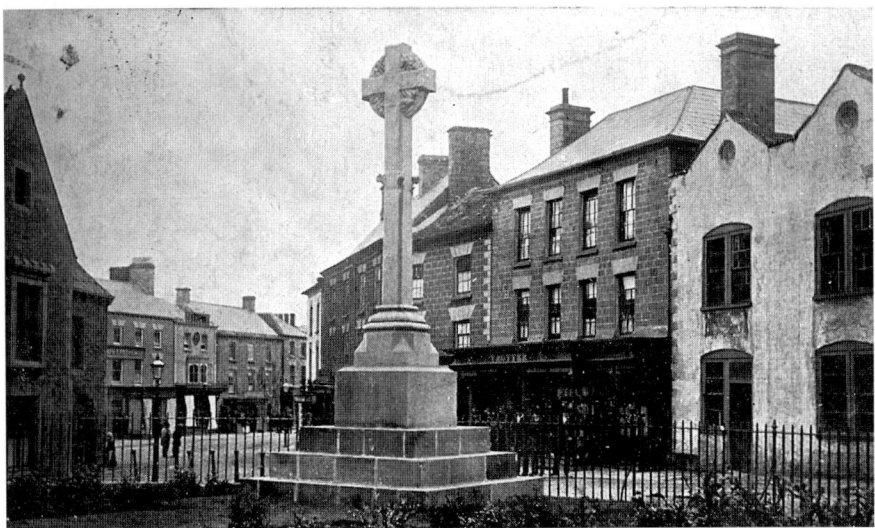

The 'modern' cross erected to mark the position of the old Coleford church, as photographed by John Prter around 1900.

DEERHURST. Glos.
NGR SO 870299 Sheet 162
Missing.

Deerhurst, now a quiet village, was an important place in Saxon times and the first church probably dates from the 7th century or earlier. Inside the Priory Church a Saxon font stands on an ornamented pillar which some say is part of a Saxon cross – and both have a story to tell. The font was found in a farmyard doing service as a washtub whilst the base was found in a garden close to the river.

Even when Charles Pooley published his work on the Old Crosses of Gloucestershire in 1868, the cross which stood in the village had long disappeared. It would be interesting to know where it had stood and what its appearance had been.

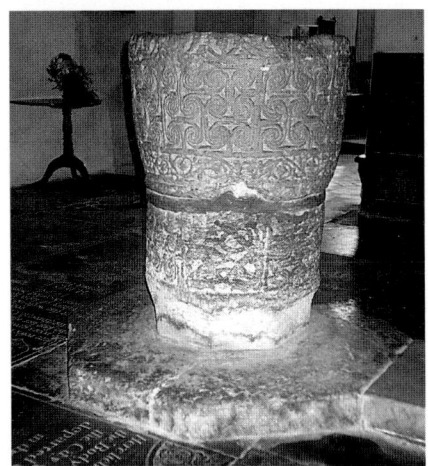

The font in Deerhurst Church standing on an ornamented pillar, said to be part of a cross.

DIXTON. Mon.

NGR SO 520135 Sheet 162

This graceful, restored cross stands on a step near the tower. The octagonal base has broaches out of which rises the shaft, only the lower part is ancient, the upper part with the head being modern. When this churchyard was first visited twenty years ago there was a second carved, octagonal base on the south side of the church, said to have come from the church of St Thomas, Wyesham. However, when we again called there in 1993 only a plain square stone with a socket remained. It was later learned that the stone is now in the garden of the Army Museum, Monmouth Castle, where it had been taken for safety.

Of course Monmouth also has a restored cross set in the middle of the roundabout at Over Monnow – the elaborate head of which was recently missing for some time, but is now back in place.

There was another monument known as White Cross which stood approximately where the War Memorial and tree are in White Cross Street. From a recently acquired print, it appears to have been a Latin cross on three steps, painted white.

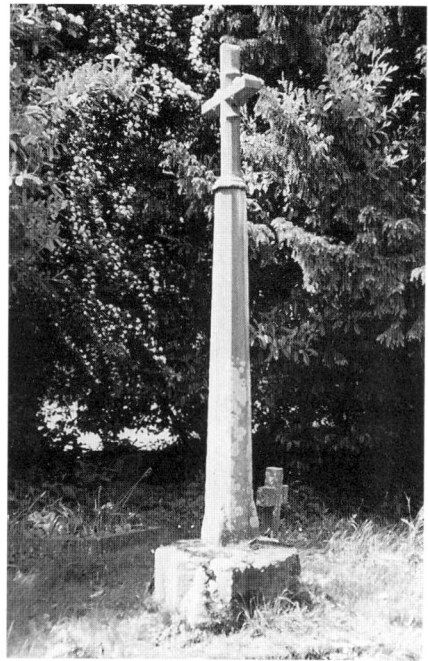

Churchyard Cross, Dixton.

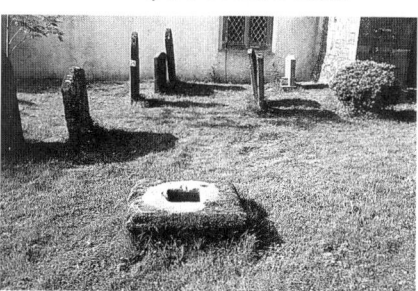

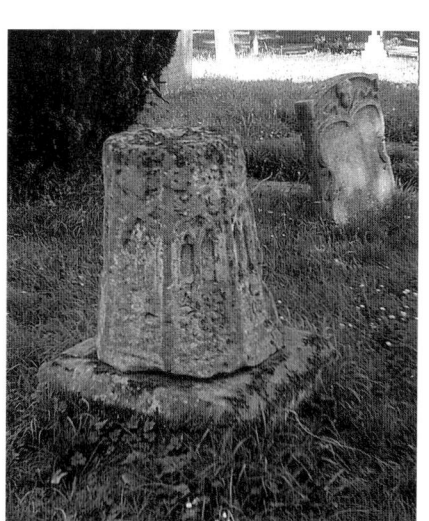

A base stone in the churchyard at Dixton which is believed to have come from St. Thomas' church, Wyesham. Originally this was complete with the base stone in the socket as seen on the left. However, the base stone has been removed to the Army Museum at Monmouth Castle as seen on the right.

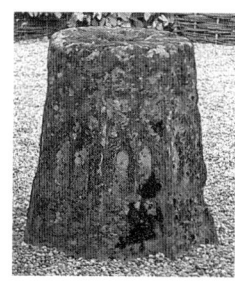

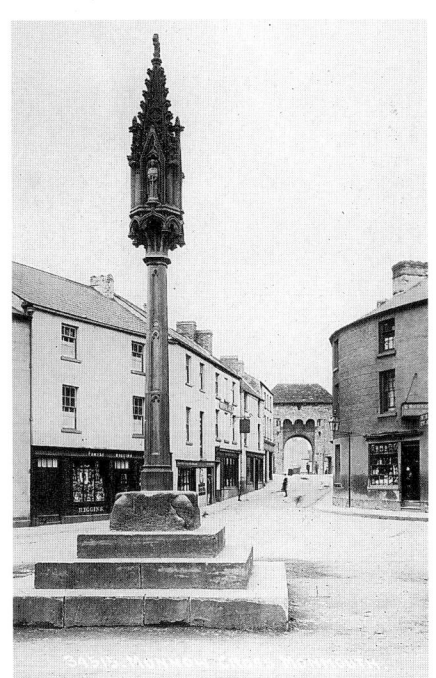
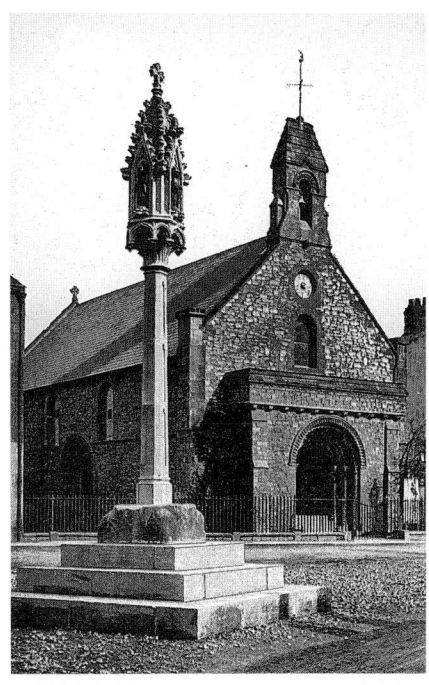
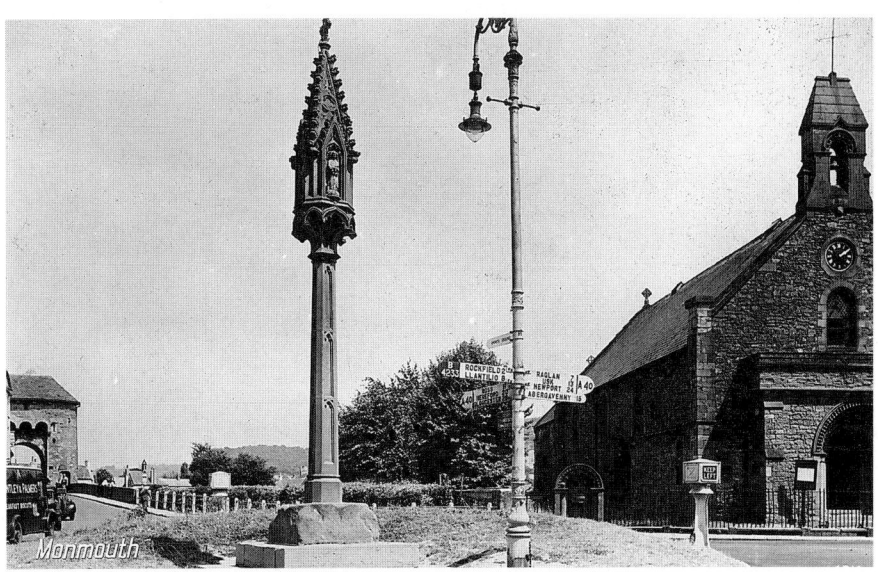

Three old postcard views of the restored cross at Over Monnow, Monmouth, ranging from about 1910 (top left) to around 1950 (bottom).

DURSLEY CROSS. Glos.
NGR SO 699201 Sheet 162

This square base lies partly buried in the grass by a fence. It was moved here by the then publican of the 'Dursley Cross Inn' (now a private house) from its position on a nearby grassy platt in order to enlarge the car park. Apparently part of it was broken in the move, but no obvious sign of a break could be seen on the visible portion. The house next to the inn had been the blacksmith shop with the green lane running up past it being Roman. The old coach road crossed the shoulder of May Hill here, and we were shown an overgrown flight of steps said to be for passengers to board or alight.

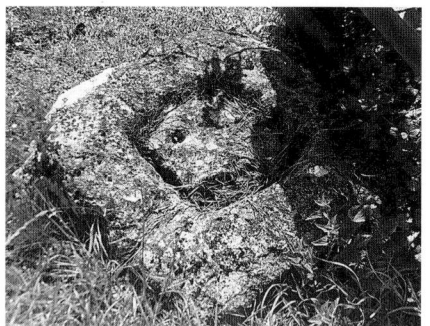

The cross base on its present site.

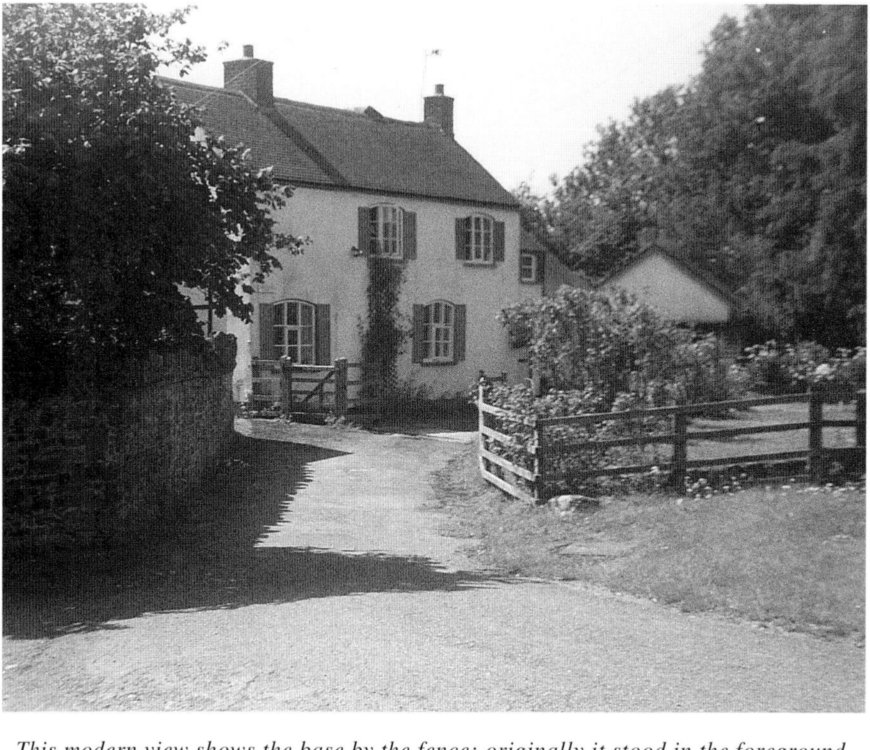

This modern view shows the base by the fence; originally it stood in the foreground.

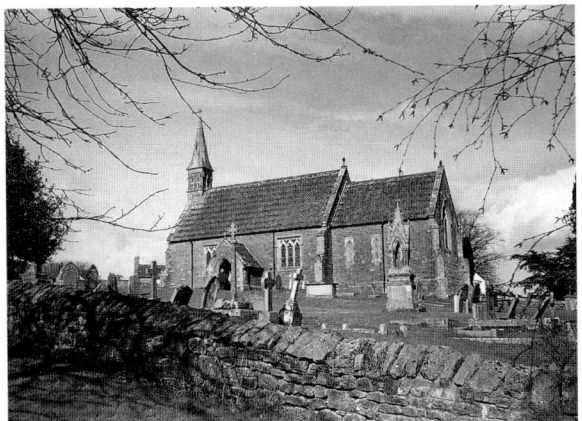

A general view of the church and churchyard, showing the cross (centre, in line with the porch) and the Albert Memorial 'look-a-like' to the right.

GANAREW. Herefs.
NGR SO 530163 Sheet 162
Churchyard.

This cross stands just inside the south-east entrance to the churchyard and consists of three steps with modern shaft and head. No socket-stone and Alfred Watkins (*The Old Standing Crosses of Herefordshire*, p44) thought it had been designed for a wooden shaft. Nearby is a very ornate structure reminiscent on a smaller scale of the Albert Memorial.

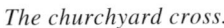

The churchyard cross.

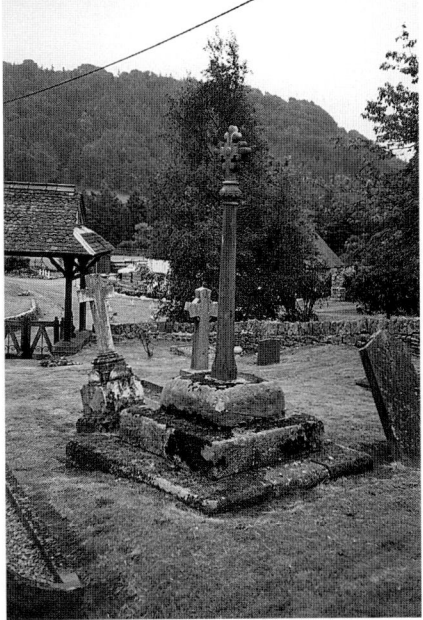

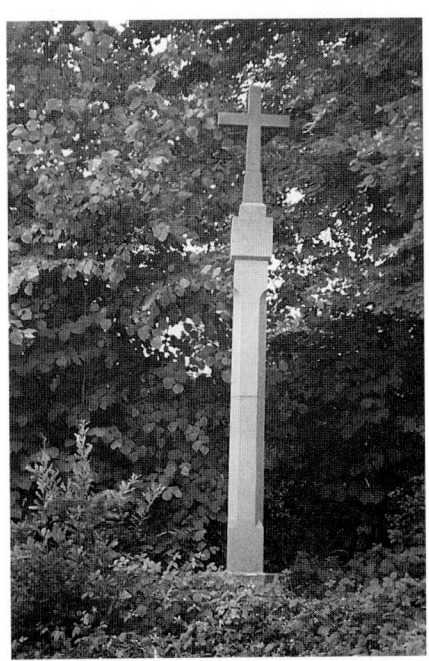

The restored wayside cross.

Wayside.
NGR SO 532163 Sheet 162

Leaving the church, one turns right across the bridge over the dual-carriageway to Ross, and at the junction the cross is seen high up on a bank with dark trees behind it, and when last seen the steps and socket-stone were covered in shrubbery. Again referring to Alfred Watkins, he said "it all seemed to be of a late date, and all above the capstone, a 'restoration'."

GOODRICH. Herefs.

NGR SO 573190 Sheet 162

The remains of this cross are opposite the south door of the church, being composed of four tiers of steps and a short length of shaft, with no socket-stone. This latter was apparently omitted during a restoration of the remains, undertaken to commemorate the coronation of George V in 1911. The shaft is square to octagonal, about 3ft. long, with stops at both ends and a square cap on the top, dated 1692, used as a sundial. Also in the churchyard on the north side is a very large boulder of conglomerate which was placed in position in memory of a Rev. Herbert. It was dragged here from the foot of Doward Hill, a traction engine being required for the purpose and part of the churchyard wall being taken down to allow access. Any plaque to this event (pre 1892) is now missing, though one can see a faint oval outline where such would have been mounted.

Goodrich Cross.

At the aptly-named crossroads, according to Alfred Watkins (p64) a cross is marked on Taylor's map of 1758, and when he first visited the site in 1919, he was told that some of the stones from the old cross were in a nearby field, but he was unable to see them. He was also informed that the milestone was part of the cross, but on examination he could see no confirmation of this fact.

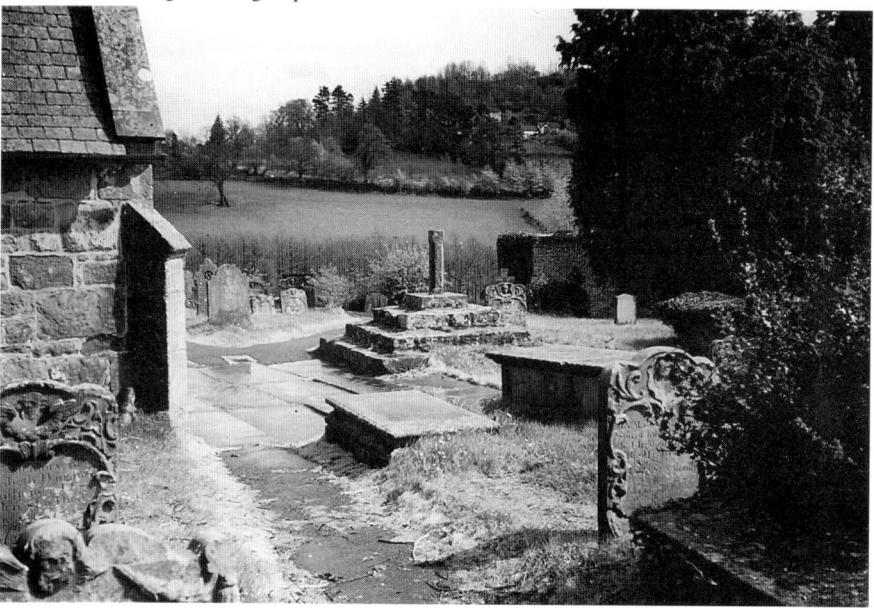

Above. *The remains of the churchyard cross.*

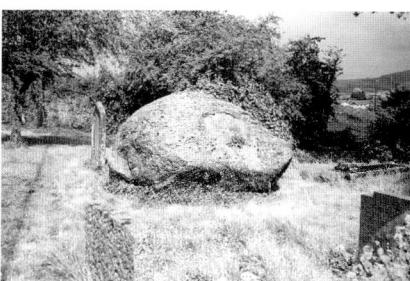

Left. *The boulder on the north side of the churchyard.*

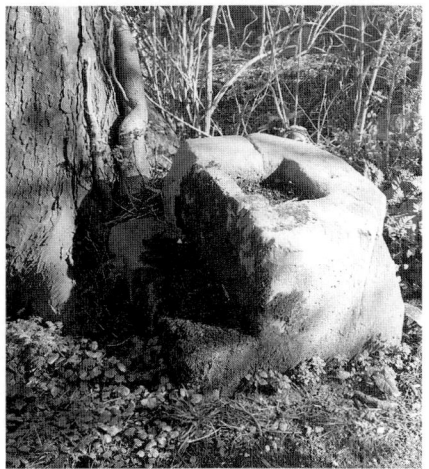

The remains of the cross base in the grounds of Hewelsfield Court.

HEWELSFIELD. Glos.

NGR SO 569022 Sheet 162.

At the entrance to Hewelsfield Court is a medieval base measuring approximately 33ins square at base. Square to octagon in its upper bed, it has been used as a mounting-block for which purpose a portion of the upper part has been cut away to form a step; and in doing so exposed the side of the socket-hole which has been built up with small stones to form a plant holder. This socket was probably 12ins square originally, but is now only 12ins by 10ins. Two of the broaches remain. Thanks were due to Mrs P. Symonds for permission to examine the stone as it is on private land.

The nearby church is largely Norman, but believed to stand on Saxon foundations; the churchyard is circular.

HOM GREEN. Herefs.

NGR SO 579221 Sheet 162

Hidden away in a private wood at Hom Green near Ross, though just visible from the nearby lane, is an elegant cross on three octagonal steps. The square socket-stone which Alfred Watkins thought could be modern and bears the name of 'Counsell', has been the model for many War Memorials. Indeed, he found it difficult to say just how much of the monument was original. The 9ft shaft, square to octagon, has pyramid corners; the capital, of good Perpendicular design, he thought could be original, while the Latin head was a modern restoration. When first seen, the monument was surrounded by a sea of snowdrops - a lovely sight. As Watkins records, there is no sign of a church on the site, but he had heard rumours of some foundations having been seen near it.

On the opposite side of the road is the boarded-up Hom Church standing in a very overgrown churchyard.

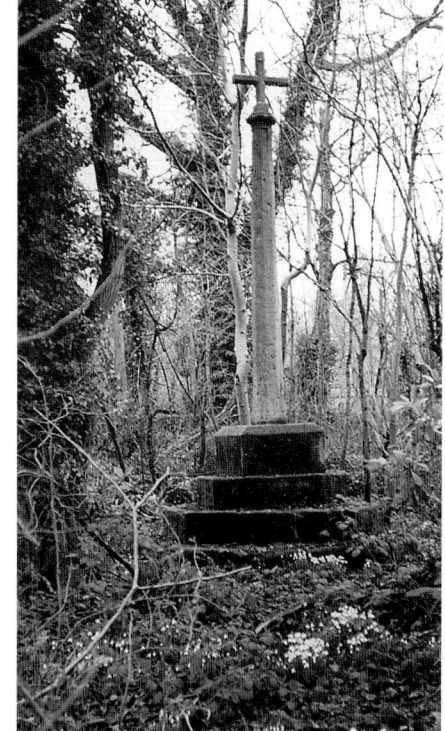

The restored cross in the wood, Hom Green.

HUNTLEY.

NGR SO 723194 Sheet 162

Also known as the 'Black Stone', this rough base with a portion of its shaft still in the socket, stands in North Road, near the public telephone box.

Again, this one was not recorded by Charles Pooley in 1868.

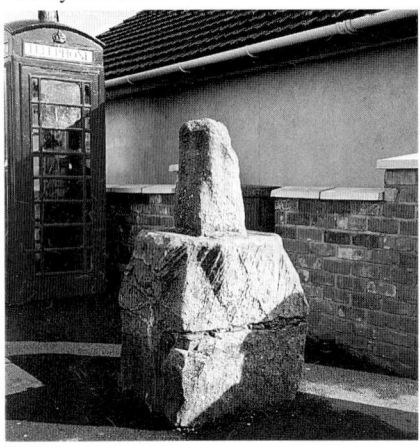

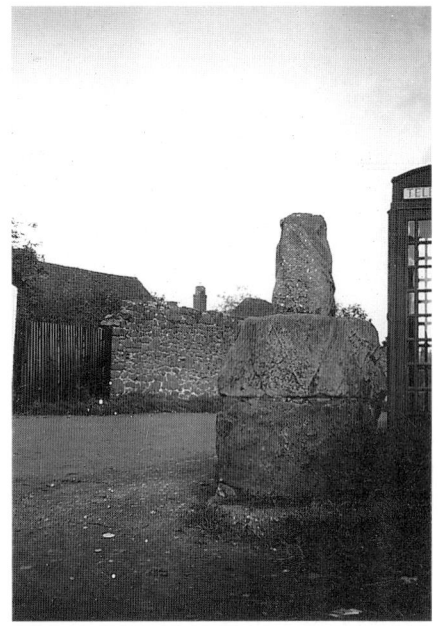

Two views of the 'Black Stone', Huntley.

KEMPLEY. Glos.

NGR SO 670312 Sheet 162

In the vestry under the tower of the delightful, though now redundant, church of St Mary's can be seen a rough Norman gable cross. According to the church notes, 'In the vestry is seen a crude Saxon Cross found in 1912 when the tower floor was repaired.' The gable cross on the east end of the chancel appears not unlike that preserved in the vestry. The church is renowned for the splendid medieval wall paintings inside.

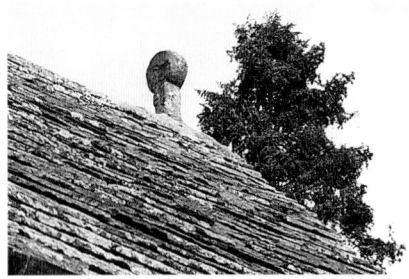

The gable cross on the east end of the church.

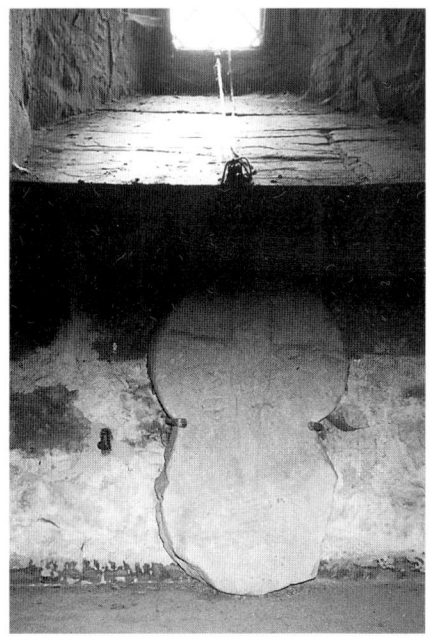

The gable cross in the vestry.

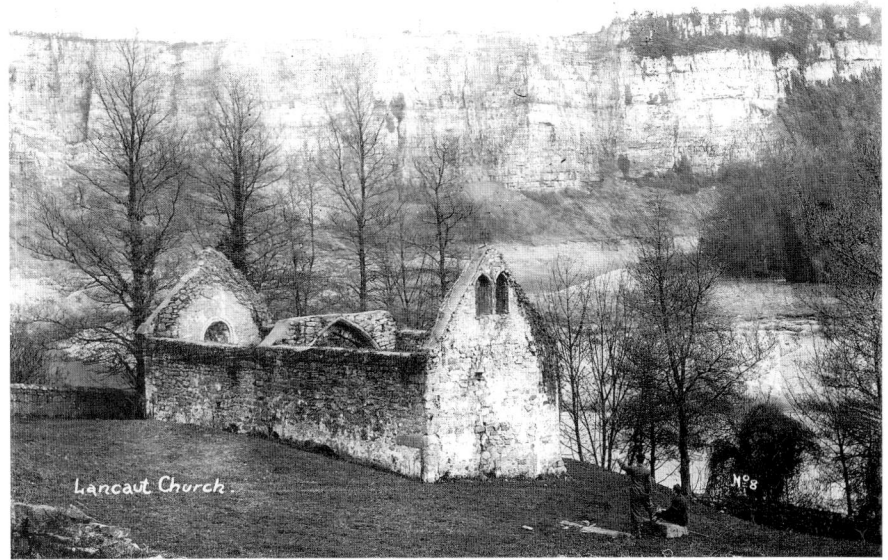

The remains of Lancaut Church photographed around 1930.

LANCAUT. Glos.

NGR 536964 Sheet 162

The ruined church of St James is situated close to the River Wye. The square socket-stone lies fairly deeply embedded in the ground at the west end of the church, with two other stones nearby which may have been part of the original structure. There is the remains of the shaft, broken off level with the top of the stone, in the socket-hole. The Norman lead font from St James is now in the Lady Chapel in Gloucester Cathedral.

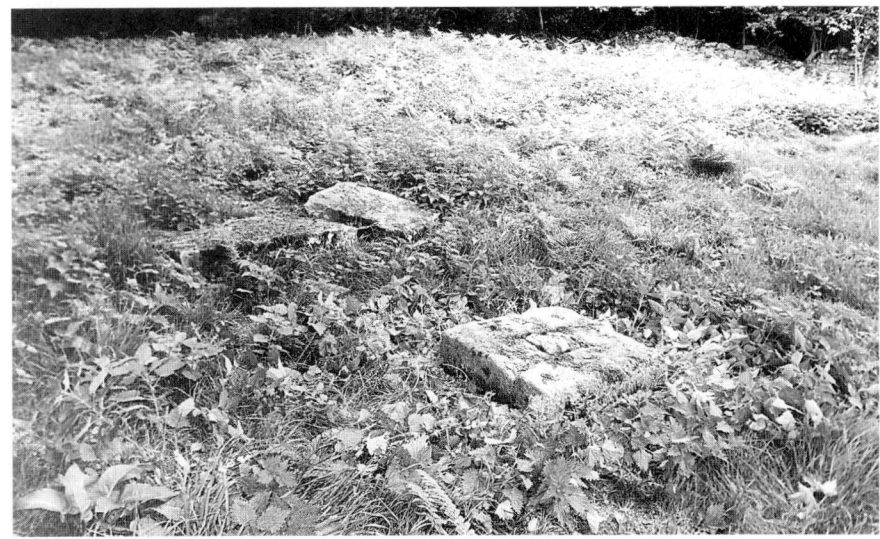

Remains of the cross base, together with stones which may have been part of the original structure.

LITTLEDEAN. Glos.

NGR SO 668137 Sheet 162

While searching for any remains of the Littledean Market Cross mentioned in a 1920s guide book as having been removed to the grounds of Flaxley Grange, the writer eventually made contact with Mrs J. Felton of Littledean House Hotel, in the grounds of which is a portion of the head of a cross. This cross-head appears to be like the lantern-type, approximately 38ins high with octagonal sides of 10ins and 8ins alternately. The heads of the figures in the niches have been broken off and the whole monument is rather weather-worn. Littledean Cross was taken down in 1821 having become a traffic hazard and removed to the grounds of the Grange; later in the 1890s it was again removed, this time to a garden in Newnham. This fragment of Littledean Market Cross was eventually traced to the Grange (now Grange Village), Newnham. About 30 years ago when Mr. John Canning and his wife came there, it was still standing in the grounds but on an approach from interested persons in Littledean, it was returned and is that now in the Littledean House Hotel grounds. The writer was fortunate enough to meet the late Mr. H. Boughton, then of Mitcheldean but who had previously farmed at Littledean, who had a framed drawing of the Littledean Market Cross which he kindly allowed to be photographed. It was a low-roofed structure on pillars with four or five steps of the cross underneath, and topped by a tall Gothic pinnacle with niches and figures – the portion now in the hotel grounds. The original site is now marked by a small traffic island. Some people think it is part of 'Nightingale Cross' which marked the parish boundary close by, but this is apparently a mistaken idea, which leaves the question as to what became of Nightingale Cross?

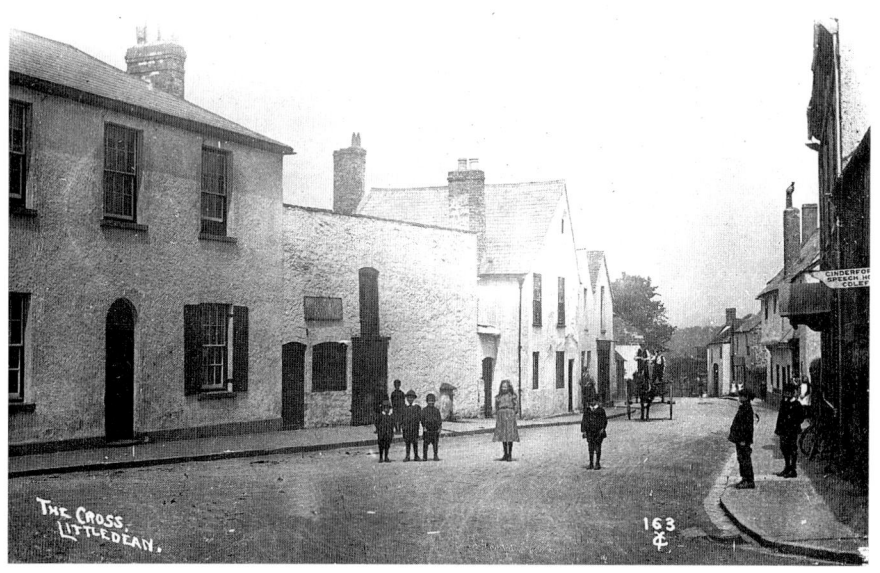

The site of Littledean Cross, on an old postcard of around 1905.

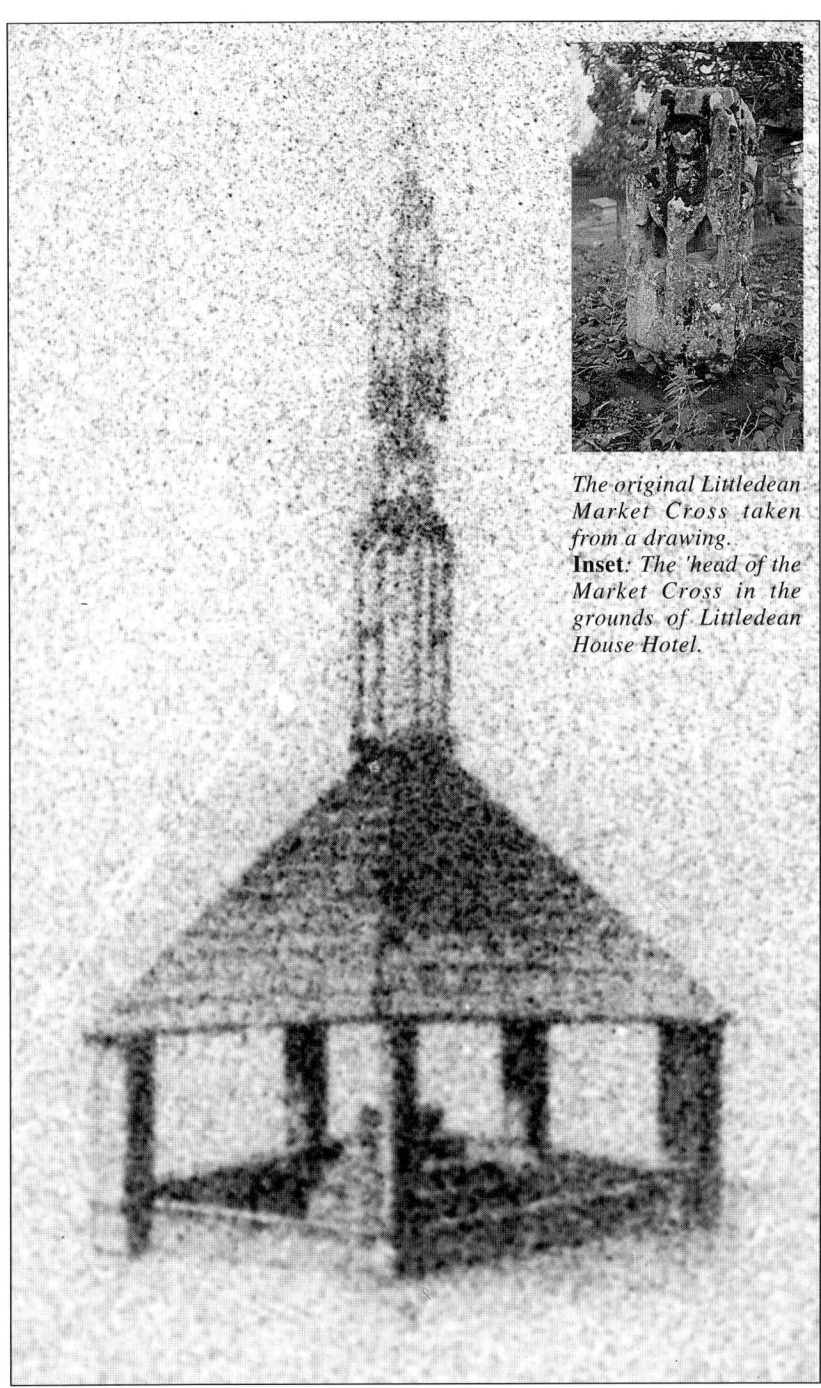

The original Littledean Market Cross taken from a drawing.
Inset: *The 'head of the Market Cross in the grounds of Littledean House Hotel.*

LONGHOPE. Glos.

NGR SO 685198 Sheet 162

Churchyard. There are two bases in Longhope village, the wayside one and that in the churchyard. The latter is near the south entrance to the church and stands on what appears to be a fallen tombstone. It is square to octagon above, and measures approximately 23ins square at the bottom, and is 16ins deep. When first seen, there was a stone mortar on top which had served as a font from the 1660s when the medieval one had been destroyed by order of Parliament, until the present one was placed in the church in 1860; however, this mortar has now disappeared.

Wayside.

NGR SO 693186 Sheet 162

This is a large square base octagonal above, set on a built-up step of small stones, on a lower step, and stands opposite the War Memorial. The shaft has been cut off level with the top of the stone and had been leaded into the socket. This monument has obviously been re-erected, possibly due to road alterations.

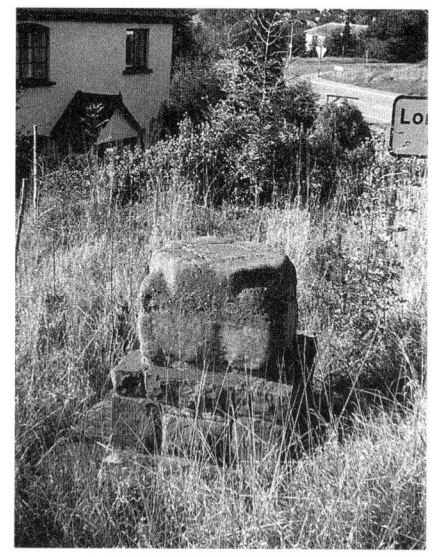

The wayside cross, Longhope.

Below. *The base in Longhope churchyard.*

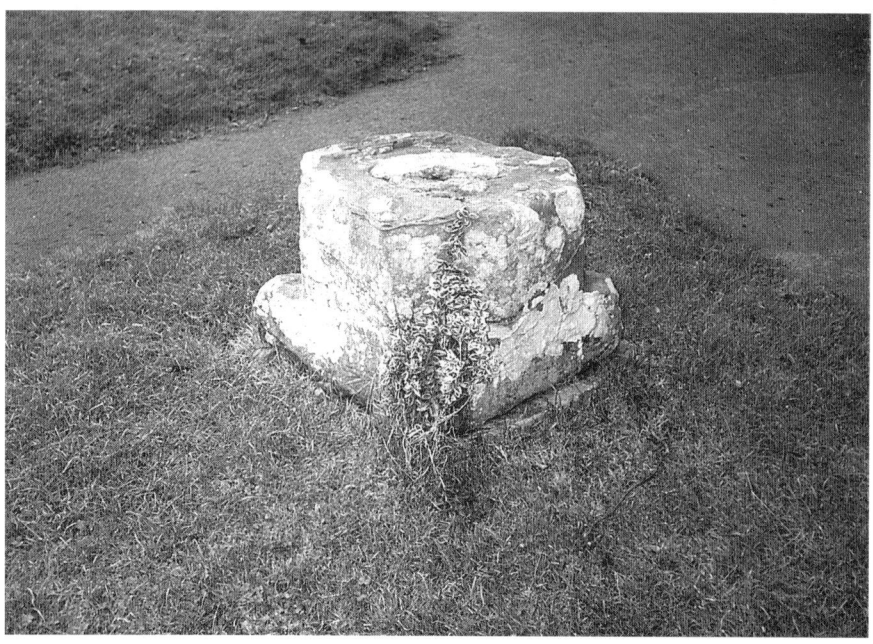

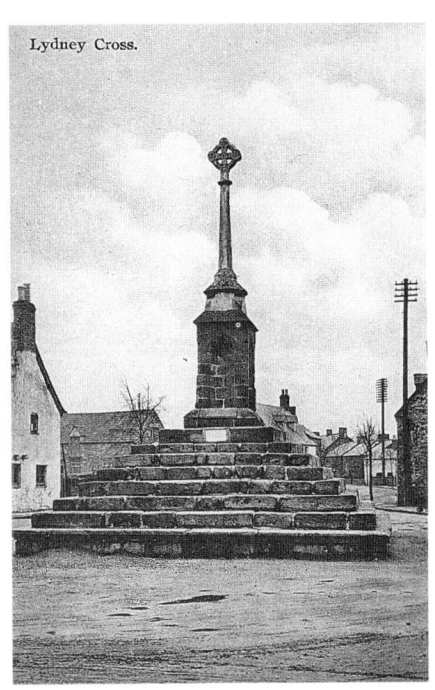

Lydney Cross.

LYDNEY. Glos.
NGR SO 630028 Sheet 162
Ancient Monument.
This fine, restored cross stands in situ by the side of the A48 road at the top of Church Street in the area known as 'The Cross' because of its presence. Like those of Aylburton and Clearwell, it belongs to the early 14th century, and is the largest of the three, being just over 24ft at the base and having eight steps. For many years there was only the shrine with its four niches on each side, on top of the steps, until it was restored in 1878 as a memorial to the Rev. W. H. Bathurst of Lydney Park, by his family.

Two views of Lydney Cross, taken from old postcards, dating from before the First World War.

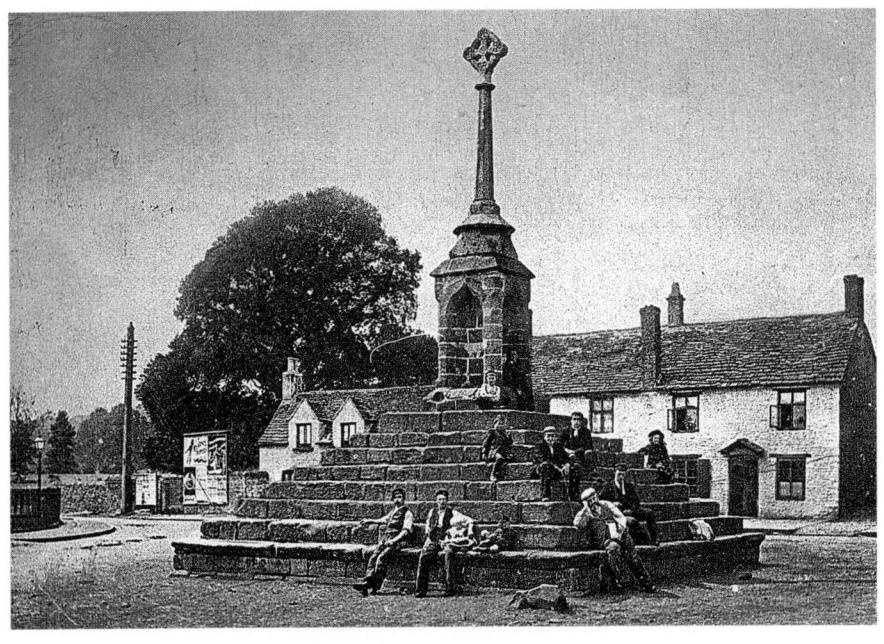

MAISEMORE. Glos.

NGR SO 814216 Sheet 162

The remains of the churchyard cross, consisting of three steps and a small portion of the shaft, stands on the south side of the church. The lower step is nearly level with the surrounding grass, and the shaft has practically crumbled away.

Maisemore Bridge.

NGR SO 818211 Sheet 162

The 1785 bridge at Maisemore was replaced in 1956 by a concrete structure, and at its eastern approach is a 19th century cross with the following inscription: 'This Cross was taken from St Michael's Church, Gloucester, in 1956.' An older cross once stood on an earlier bridge built circa 1200 and carried an inscription in Latin and Norman-French: 'In honour of Our Lord Jesus Christ who was crucified for us. William Fitz Anketill of Lilton made this Cross and the same William Fitz Anketill began this bridge of Maisemore.' Charles Pooley refers to 'a curious cross which once stood on old Maisemore Bridge.'

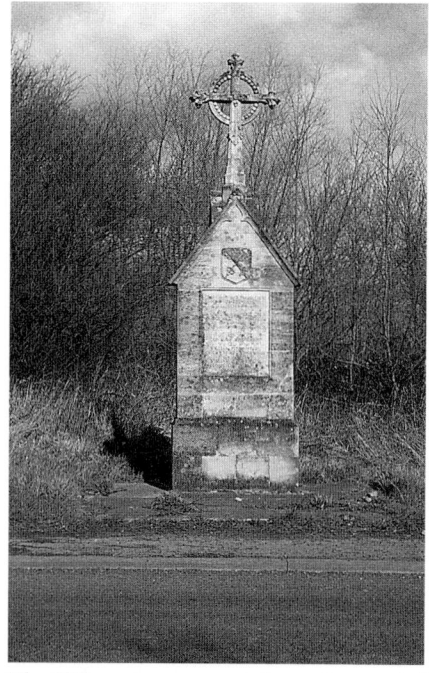

The 19th century cross at the eastern end of Maisemore Bridge.

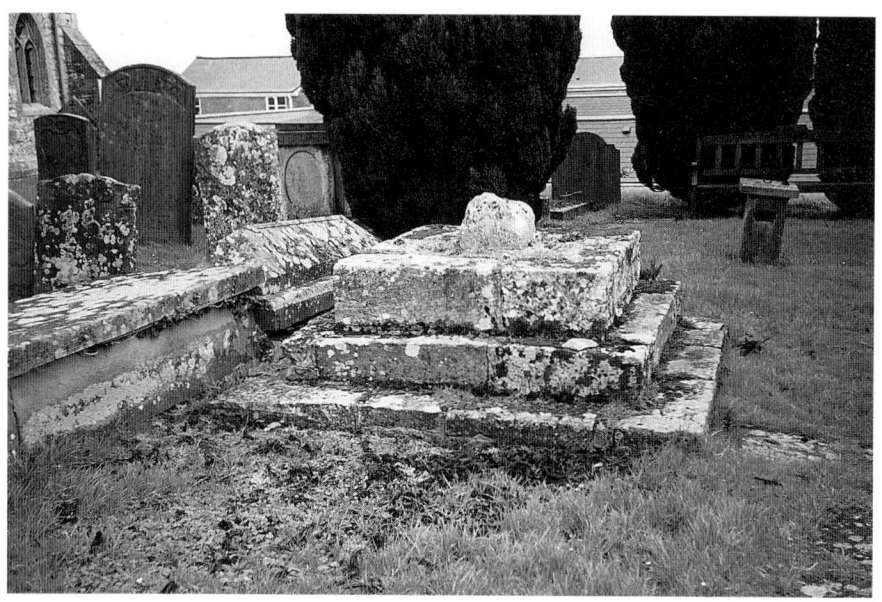

Remains of the churchyard cross.

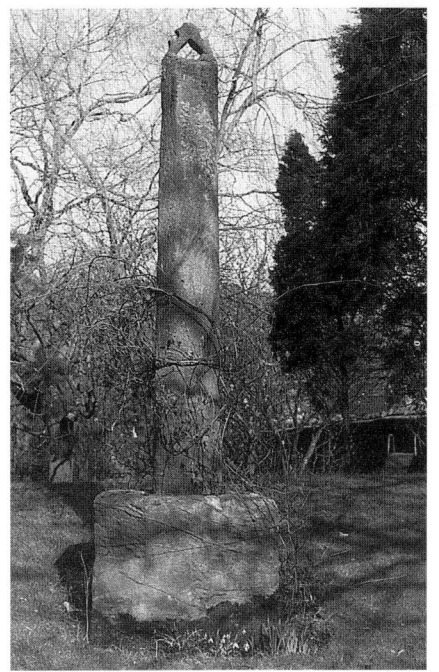

MITCHELDEAN. Glos.
NGR SO 666184 Sheet 162

Merend Cross. The only remains found to date are those of Merend Cross noted in 1576, and now in a garden alongside the Gloucester road, where it was placed when removed from its original site on the Abenhall boundary. It consists of a large square base with deep shoulders at the top. When seen in 1988 there was a piece of carving placed on the top of the shaft - part of the head? The tall shaft appears to have been broken at some time.

There were other crosses at various places in the streets; the High Cross, noted in 1548, stood outside the church; in 1750 it bore a clock but was rebuilt in 1775, this building being pulled down during last century. There was also a Market Cross in 1548 replaced in 1710 by a Market House, which in turn was rebuilt as the Town Hall in 1816. The site of the Butter Cross dating from before 1686 and demolished in 1775, is unknown.

Remains of the Merend Cross, now in a private garden.

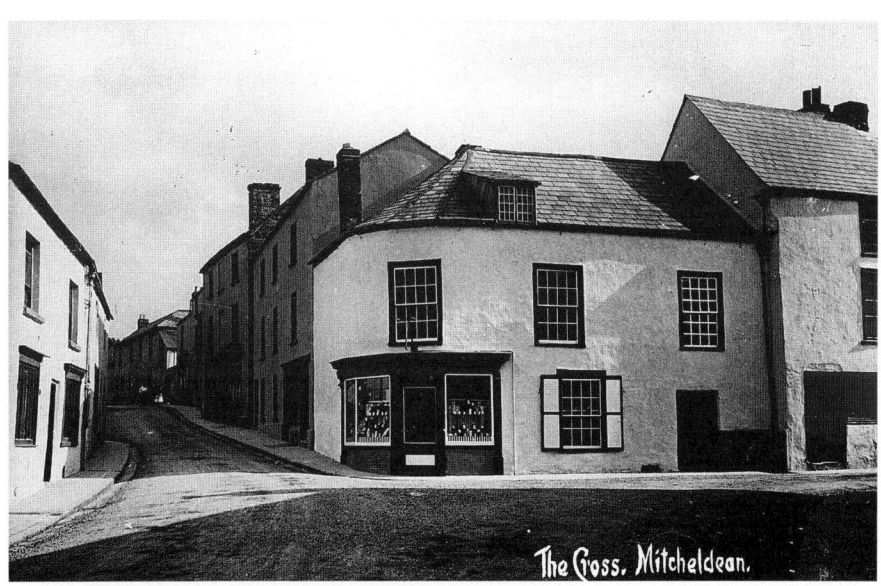

A c1930 view of The Cross from an old postcard by Gibbs of Cinderford.

25

NEWENT. Glos.

NGR SO 724259 Sheet 162

In Church. In the south porch of the church stands part of a sculptured Anglo-Saxon cross-shaft, found in the churchyard in 1907. Probably of the early 9th century, it is one of the oldest stone crosses in Gloucestershire. On it are depicted the 'Sacrifice of Isaac', 'David and Goliath' and the 'Fall of Man' with Adam and Eve standing either side of the Tree of Knowledge around which is entwined the Serpent.

Market Hall or Butter Cross.
Ancient Monument.

Market crosses probably developed from the usual cross-on-steps type with the demand for greater comfort and convenience of the people gathered around it for market business. 'This demand was met by erecting a penthouse roof about the lower part of the existing cross.' (Vallance, *Old Crosses & Lychgates*, 1920). This cannot have been a very successful solution as it would only have sheltered a very few, and eventually the market cross evolved such as that at Newent where many more could shelter beneath its roof, while the upper floor could be used for storage or local business.

In the centre of the town is the Market or Town Hall, or, as F W Baty says in his book, *Forest of Dean*, Butter Cross, and which he says 'is the only such building in our area standing on legs.' Other sources refer to it as a restored late 16th or 17th century timber-framed building with one large room approached by outside stairs and supported on twelve posts. It was built as the Butter Market in 1668 and is listed as an Ancient Monument (No.114). It was thoroughly restored by Richard Foley Onslow Esq., in 1864. In January 1991 it was the subject of an appeal by the Mayor of Newent to save it; it is pleasant to relate that the restoration was completed in May 1991 and it is now a special feature of that area.

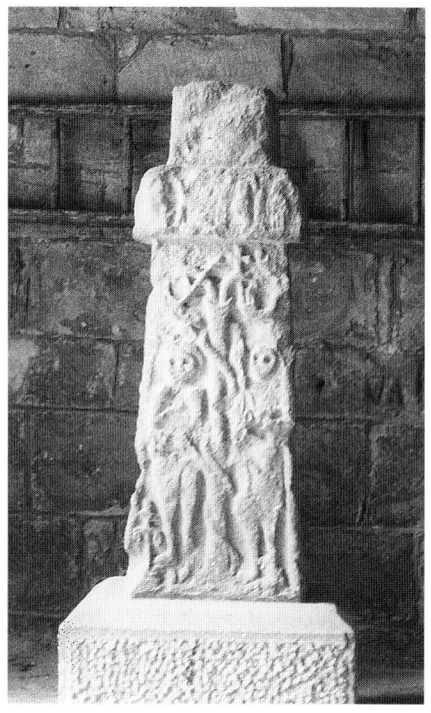

Remains of Saxon cross-shaft in church porch.

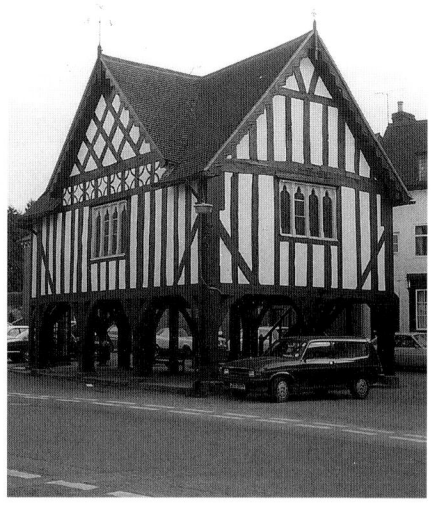

Market Hall, or Butter Cross, town centre.

NEWLAND. Glos.

NGR SO 553095 Sheet 162

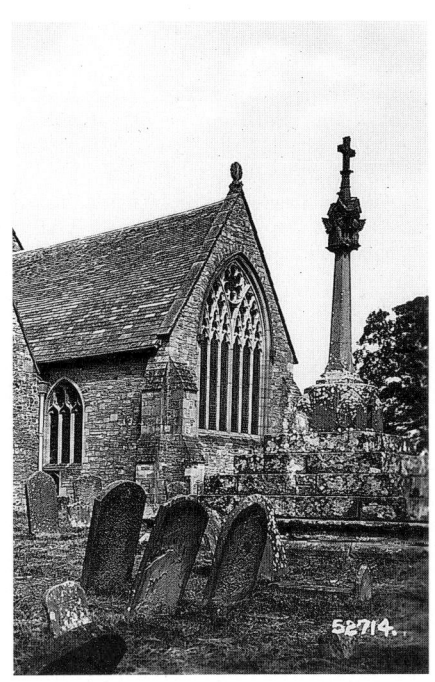

In the churchyard stands the 14th century cross; standing on the original five steps, the rest of it is modern, having been restored in memory of Margaret Birt, 1864. The old socket-stone, which was found to be in too poor a state to be re-used at that time, was put together as well as possible and stands nearby.

The ancient church of All Saints, Newland, contains not only the famous Miner's Brass, but also the ornate tomb of Jenkyn Wyrall which originally stood in the churchyard but was brought into the church in 1950 to preserve it from further weathering. Also in the church can be seen the Archer tomb, a flat slab showing a bowman complete with his bow, horn and dagger thought to have been one of the King's bowbearers – probably from the style of costume, it can be dated to the early 17th century.

Left. *Restored cross in churchyard.*

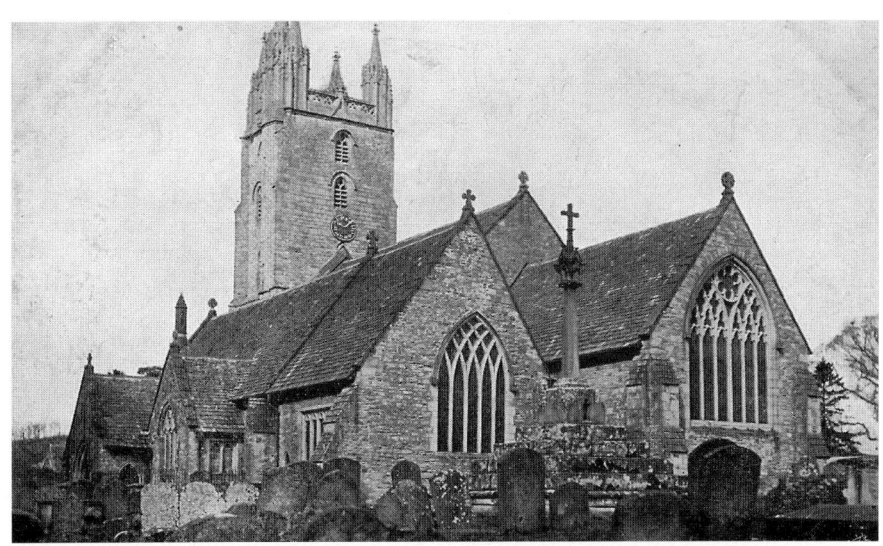

All Saints Church, Newland, around 1905, with the cross prominent.

NEWNHAM-ON-SEVERN. Glos.
Missing.
approximate NGR SO 691117 Sheet 162

The High Cross, mentioned in 1540, stood at the crossroads in the centre of the town where the road from the Forest of Dean leads down to the river, crossing the main road from Gloucester to South Wales. The church of St. Peter, Newnham, restored twice last century, contains the Norman font and part of a tympanum showing the Tree of Life. Both of these probably came from the ancient church which stood on The Nab and was washed away by a change in the course of the river Severn. In the north porch is a gable cross most probably of Victorian date.

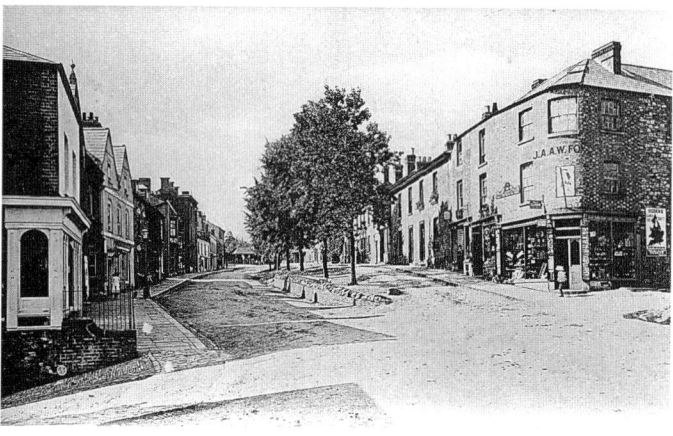

The site of the High Cross, Newnham, on an old postcard from about 1910.

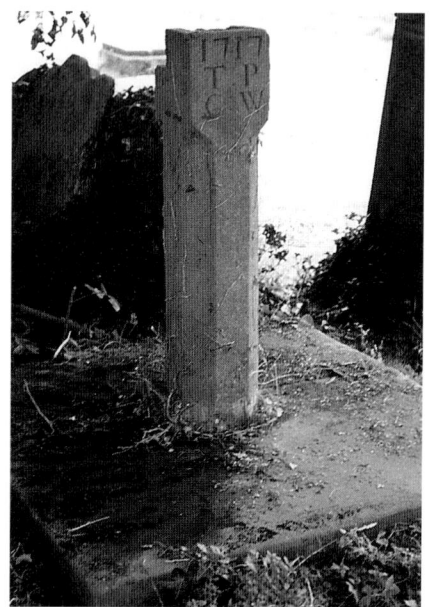

Shaft and base in the churchyard.

OXENHALL. Glos.
NGR SO 711266 Sheet 162

Sheltered by a giant yew, this monument stands on the south side of the church opposite the church doorway. When first seen, it appeared to be a tomb completely covered in ivy and brambles; but both the site and its shape gave its true identity. After clearing, it was revealed as a base, 46ins square made up of three stones 3ins deep on top of small stones. The larger of the three stones is 27ins wide, with the other two being approximately 23ins each and they are all joined together with iron clamps. The shaft is octagonal and $36^1/_2$ins high, with only $32^1/_2$ins on one side where part has been cut away. It has apparently been used for a sundial and on one side facing the church, in three lines, are the following figures and letters: 1717; T.P; C. W. Thomas Pitt was churchwarden and Parish Clerk from 1713 so the initials are probably his. Not recorded by Charles Pooley.

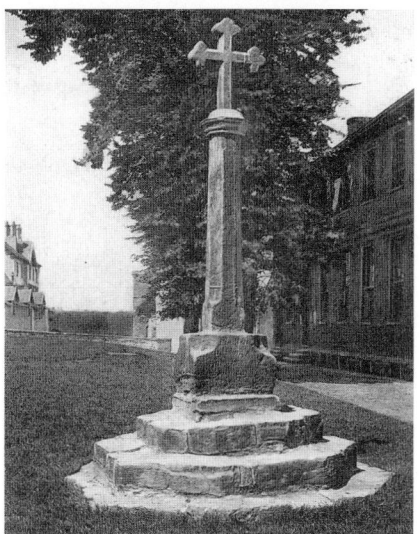

The Plague Cross in the churchyard, c1910.

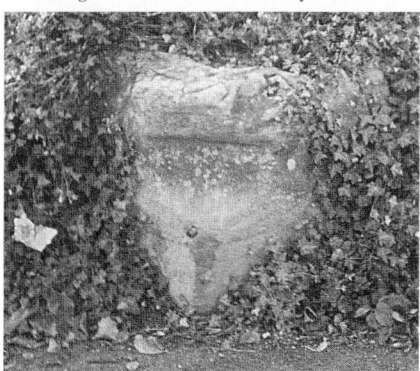

Base of the Edde Cross.

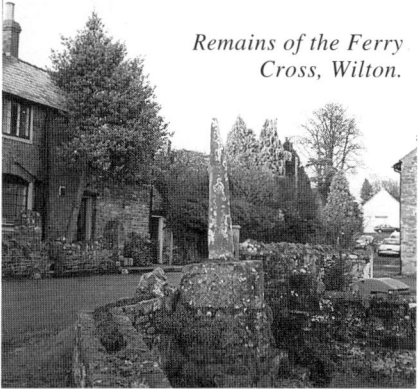

Remains of the Ferry Cross, Wilton.

ROSS ON WYE. Herefs.

Ross had three crosses in the old days, but now there are only two.

Churchyard.

NGR SO 598241 Sheet 162

One is that restored in the churchyard and known as the Plague Cross having been used as a memorial to the dead who were buried in a pit to the west of it. It is 14th century and stands on three octagonal steps with the base stone inscribed: *'Plague, Anno. Dom. 1637, Burials 315. Libera nos Domine.'* The shaft, which is square to octagonal and 5ft 6ins high, is probably original, but the head is modern.

Edde Cross.

NGR SO598242 Sheet 162

Only the socket-stone of this monument remains, which stood at the junction of Edde Cross Street but is now on a wall at the top of Wye Street, where it is practically overgrown with ivy – perhaps this is no bad thing as it may help to protect it from being removed. It is also square to octagon and like the churchyard cross is of the early 14th century.

The third cross was possibly in the aptly-named Corpse Cross Street (Alfred Watkins, p55), but the writer has found no trace of it to date.

Wilton.

NGR SO 587242 Sheet 162

While in the Ross vicinity, across the river Wye at Wilton the weather-worn remains of the Ferry Cross are to be found in a garden beside the road. The basement which is modern, supports the square socket-stone with bevelled corners, and is 3ft 2ins by 2ft high. The broken-topped shaft is square to octagon and about 7ft high. Alfred Watkins (*The Old Straight Track*, 1978 ed. p23), referring to Mark Stones, says: 'There was often one at a ford or ferry, and this sometimes developed into a ferry cross as at Wilton.'

RUDFORD. Glos.

NGR SO 773222 Sheet 162

Barbers Bridge. Although not an ancient cross, this monument is of interest and is therefore included in this work. Standing high on the edge of the road cutting at Barbers Bridge, Rudford, on the B4215 Gloucester-Newent road, is a 19th century memorial made partly with stones from the ancient walls of the city of Gloucester. It commemorates the 500 Welsh bowmen who were killed on 24th March 1643 when attacked by Colonel Massey and Sir William Waller. A local tradition held that this was the place where the Welshmen were surprised and slain; and in 1868, when a mound of earth was removed to fill a nearby pond, a large number of skeletons were discovered. They were re-buried and the 20ft obelisk surmounted by a Latin cross was erected at the expense of Mr. W. P. Price in 1871. It bears the following inscription: 'These stones, taken from the ancient walls of the city of Gloucester, mark the burial place of the Welsh of Lord Herbert's force, who fell in the combined attack by Sir William Waller and Colonel Massey on their re-entrenchment at Highnam, 24th March 1643.' There is a memorial stone set into the floor of Rudford church to the fallen. In 1970 the improvements to the B4215 road were made at this spot; however, no sign of bodies or armour was found during the excavation.

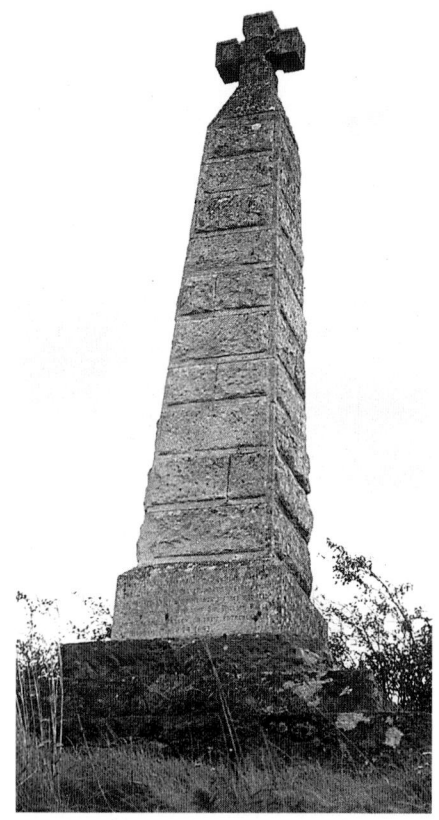

The 19th century monument on the bank at Barbers Bridge.

The following anecdote shows an amazing coincidence. Early in the 1960s my sister had occasion to visit the farm whereon this monument is sited; the farmer told her that he had recently moved there from a farm in Somerset on which a special monument existed. That one was to those who fell in the Battle of Sedgemoor, fought 6th July 1685. As he said, it was odd to have left one such object behind, to find another such here.

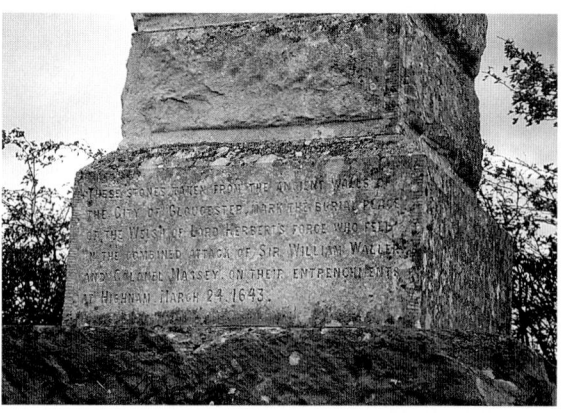

Inscription on the base of the monument.

ST. ARVANS. Mon.

NGR SO 517965 Sheet 162

Although most of the church that we see here, set back from the main Wye Valley road, dates from the 19th and 20th centuries, there are the remains of the earlier Norman building. But even this is 'modern' compared with the first church of the 10th century which had stood here. On a window-sill at the north-west end of the church is an early Christian cross-slab of the 10th century. Unfortunately, it is now in two pieces, but the Latin wheel-cross of Celtic type, filled with interlacing, and with panels of bird-headed angels on either side of it are clearly visible on the side facing out. As is mentioned on the information panel, it is interesting to note that the only other Celtic Christian monuments known in Monmouthshire (to date at least) are the cross-slabs of the same type at Balmore and Caerleon.

Right. *The broken cross-slab in the church.*

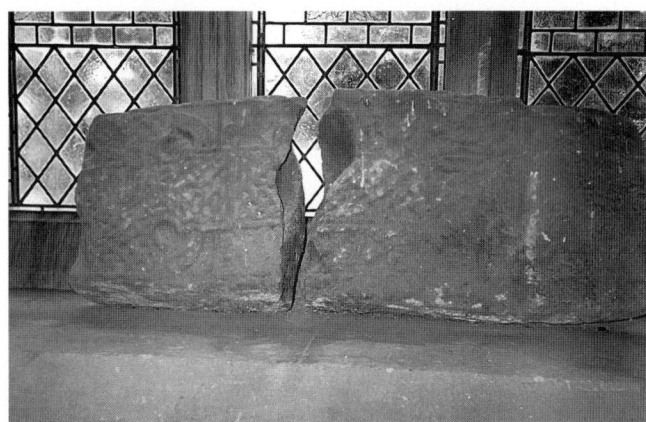

Below. *St. Arvans church.*

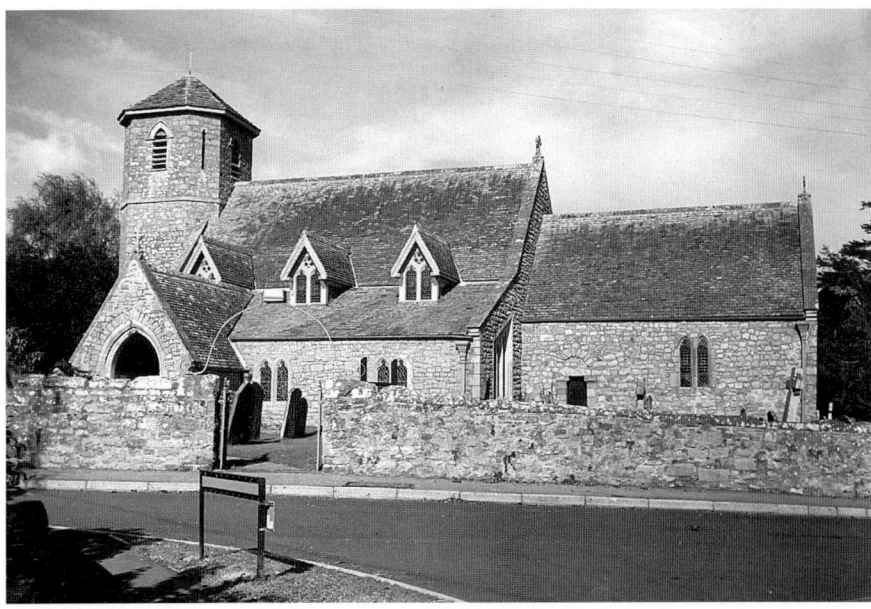

ST. BRIAVELS. Glos.
Missing.
NGR SO 559047 Sheet 162

St. Briavels had its preaching cross near the south porch but, according to Charles Pooley (p.50), it was removed in 1830 when the new tower was built. However, the church guide records this event as occurring in 1861 when the ornate box tomb of the Gough family was also removed and both were cut up and used to make the steps that lead down to the tower entrance. There were other crosses in the area – High Cross, Colpage and Whitecross near Mork, as well as Whitecross in the lower town of St. Briavels, but there are apparently no remains of any of these monuments.

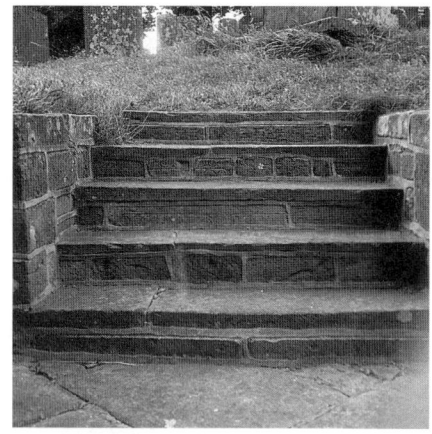

The steps to the tower entrance.

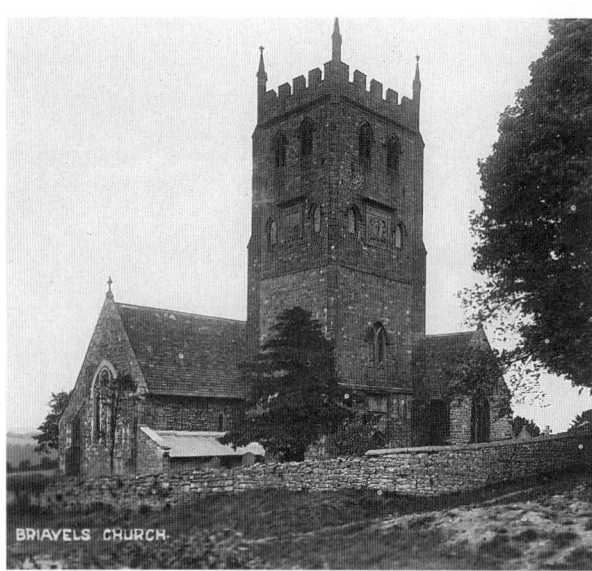

St Briavels church around 1910.

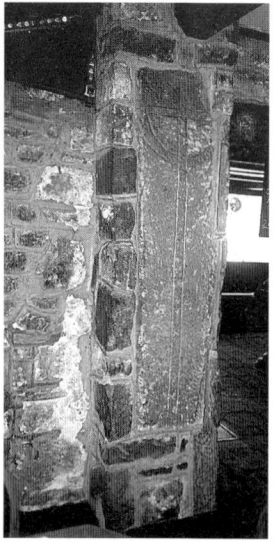

'The George Inn'.
NGR SO 559045 Sheet 162

Though not strictly a standing cross, the cross-slab now built into the bar wall of 'The George' is of great interest – probably late Saxon or early Norman. It was found during alterations serving as a lintel, and set up in its present position in 1974.

STAUNTON. Glos.

NGR SO 551126 Sheet 126

Standing on the bank opposite the church are the remains of the village cross. It consists of four octagonal steps, a large socket-stone, square at the base and octagonal above with broaches at the alternate faces. On this is an octagonal plinth into which is mortised about a foot of the shaft. It is of late 14th century date, and was repaired in 1980. The end of 1996 saw English Heritage recommending to the Secretary of State that this Grade II listed cross should be included in the Schedule of Monuments. It should then be protected as an important part of our Forest Heritage. About two hundred years ago there was another village cross here, called the 'Lower Cross', and 'possibly was near the (then) Post Office.' (B.V. Cave, n.d.) Could the upper socket-stone on the above structure have come from this cross when it was demolished?

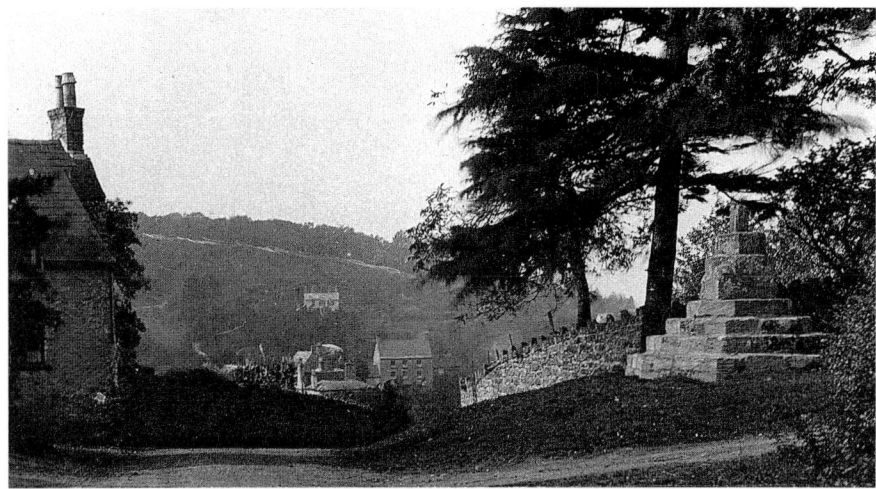

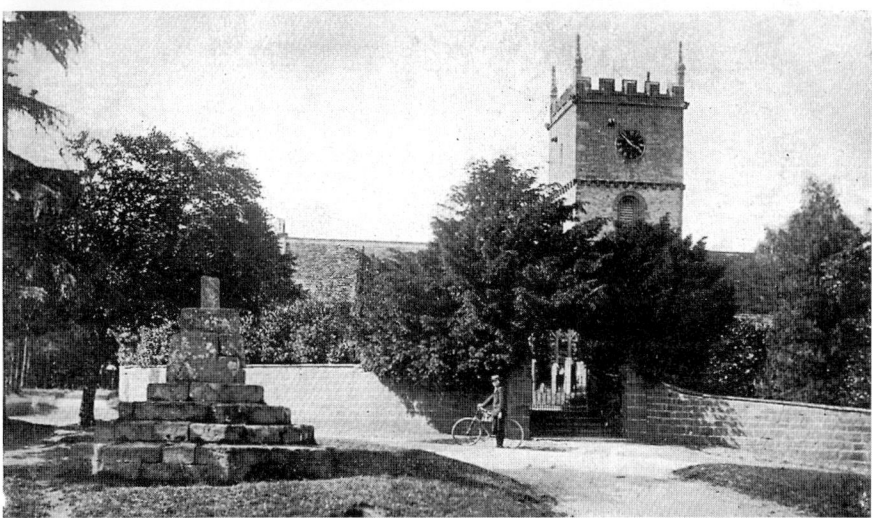

Two views of the village cross from old postcards, the top circa 1920, the lower about 1905.

TIBBERTON. Glos.

NGR SO 757219 Sheet 162

Charles Pooley recorded a portion of the octagonal shaft of a cross being preserved in the churchyard on the south side of the church. At that time it was in one piece 'rather more than 3ft' and had 'had lead inserted in a small square hole at the top, probably' as he says, 'for the union of another length of shaft.' After two failed attempts to find this fragment, it was eventually discovered at the third visit, in two pieces, lying between two box tombs. The larger portion is 24ins long and 8ins across, while the smaller is approximately 16ins long and 8ins across; the lead-filled hole being apparent in the end of the larger stone.

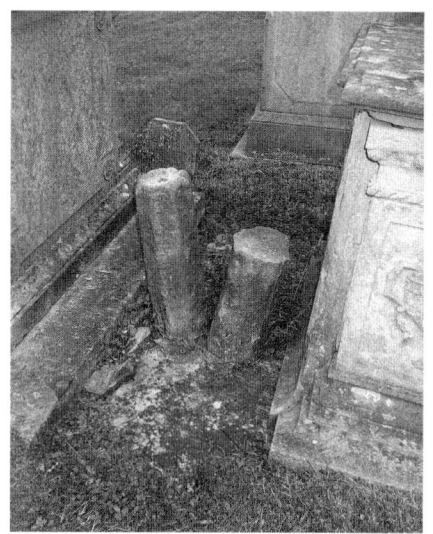

Remains of cross-shaft in churchyard.

TINTERN PARVA. Mon.

NGR SO 531008 Sheet 162

In 1893 Elizabeth Harcourt Mitchell wrote of a broken and worn base 'by the side of a lane' near the church. It was with little hopes of finding it from this rather vague description that we set off to look for it. So imagine our surprise and delight to find it – or at least, an ancient base – set on top of the pillar containing a letter box at the entrance to the lane to the church. Most of it was enveloped in ivy which we pushed back to feel for the socket-hole (it was there), and to photograph it. It is 1ft 9ins square with slight shoulders and bevelled top. Summer 1996 – Passing by one day it was pleasant to see that someone had cleared this stone of its greenery.

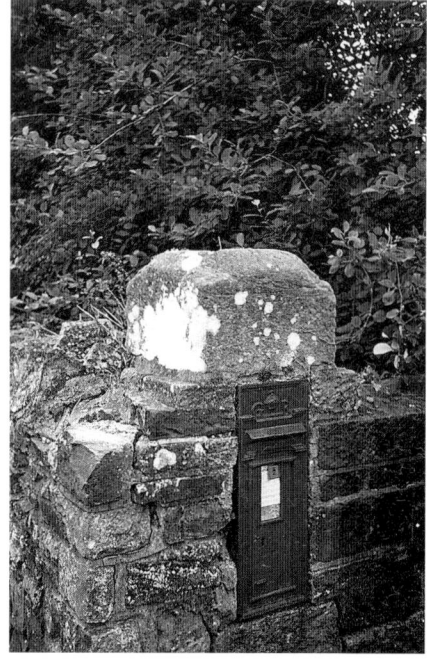

Cross base on top of wall.

TRELLECH. Mon.

NGR SO 501055 Sheet 162

Ancient Monument.

Trellech is renowned for the Harold Stones as well as the Virtuous Well, but there is a medieval preaching cross which stands in the churchyard on five steps. The socket-stone is square to octagon in its upper bed with well defined broaches at the alternate angles. Only the lower part of the shaft is original, the upper portion which tapers to the Latin cross-head, is modern.

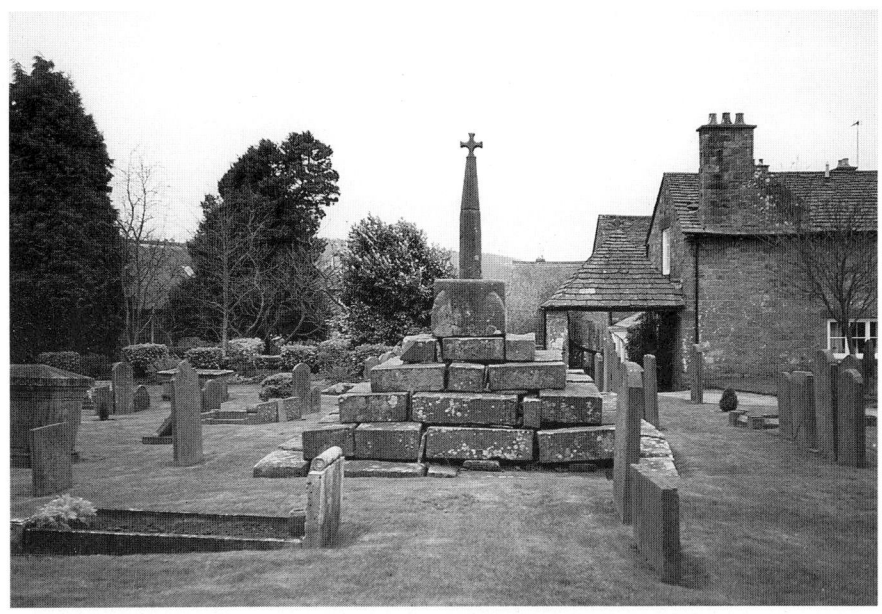

The restored churchyard cross.

TRELLECH CROSS

NGR SO 500041 Sheet 162

Ancient Monument.

Wayside.

This large medieval socket-stone, square to octagon above, stands on two steps, the lower one with an overhang, at the cross-roads south of Trellech Church. When Elizabeth Harcourt Mitchell described it in 1893, it was still used as a 'Resting Cross' by all funerals that had to pass by it.

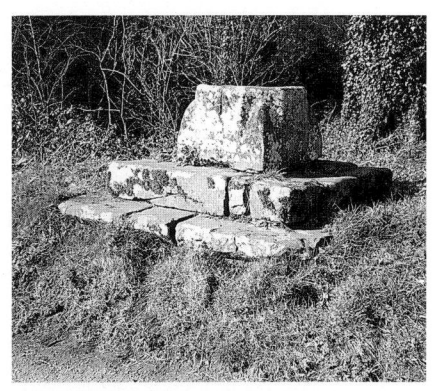

Wayside cross.

WELSH BICKNOR. Herefs.

NGR SO 592176 Sheet 162

The scramble down to, and back up from Welsh Bicknor church where it stands by the river Wye, is well worth the effort. The church was restored in the 19th century when they apparently threw out the medieval font in favour of a more 'modern' one, and at the time Arthur Mee (1938) visited the site, it lay beside the 'ancient churchyard cross.' Alfred Watkins, however, refers to the cross as 'an ornate 19th century one', while Mabel Beech (1994) calls it a very ornate Plague Cross. It has indeed a very ornate head, and where the bottom of the shaft fits into the upper portion of the 'modern' base this is topped with points. However, the lower socket-stone, square to octagon with pointed broaches, has a chamfered niche on the north side and could well be medieval in origin. It stands on three steps, the upper one with an overhanging dripstone. The Wye Valley Walk passes nearby.

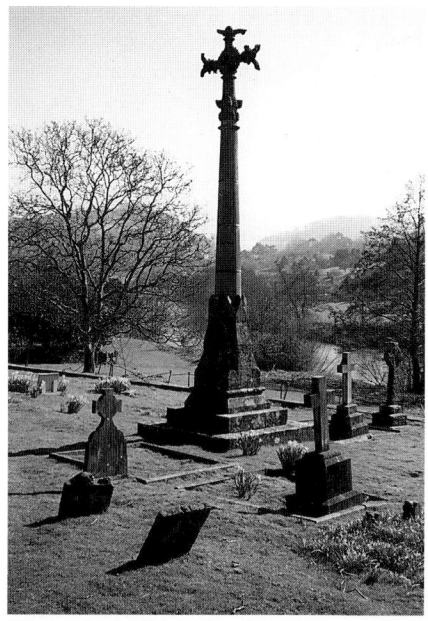

The ornate cross in the churchyard – River Wye in the background.

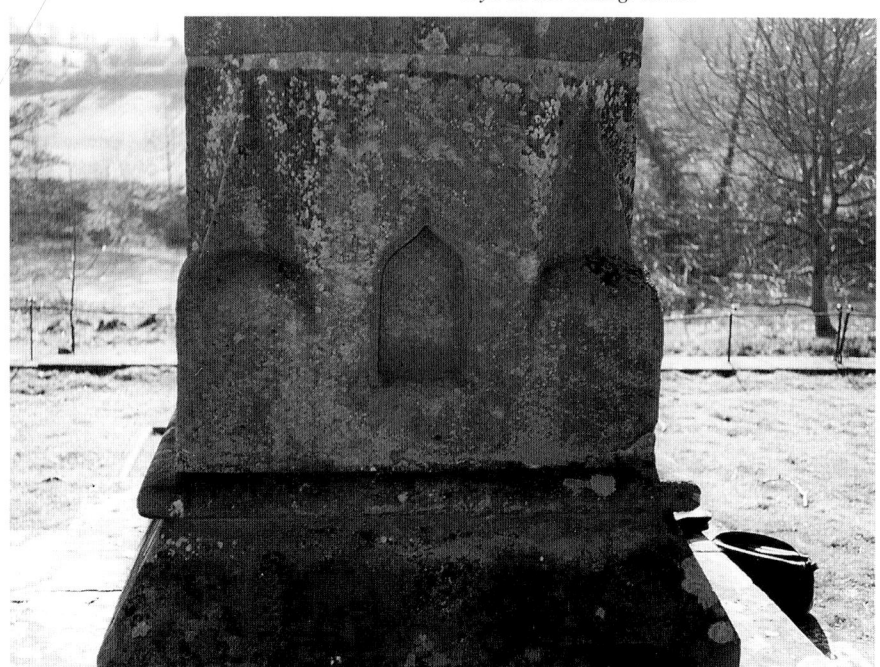

A close-up of the socket stone, showing niche.

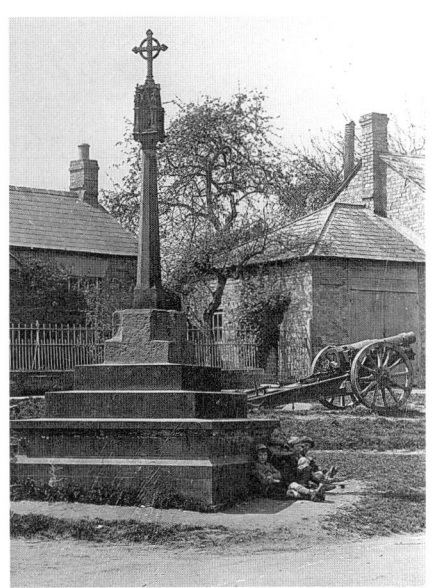

The cross around 1930.

WESTBURY ON SEVERN. Glos.

NGR SO 717140 Sheet 162

The restored village cross stands by the side of the A48; only the 12th century socket-stone, found built into the church tower during restoration work circa 1862, is original. It is square to octagon above with hollow chamfers at the corners. It was restored in 1887 to commemorate Queen Victoria's Jubilee.

Further along the road at Six Bells (*NGR SO 722138 Sheet 162*), is another base which is octagonal, although it is so worn it appears to be almost round at a brief glance. The shaft has been cut off level with the top of the stone.

In the parish is a farm called 'Broken Cross'; but on enquiry there the writer was told by the farmer that his uncle had traced the name back to circa 1320 when it was then known as 'Croft of the Brooks.'

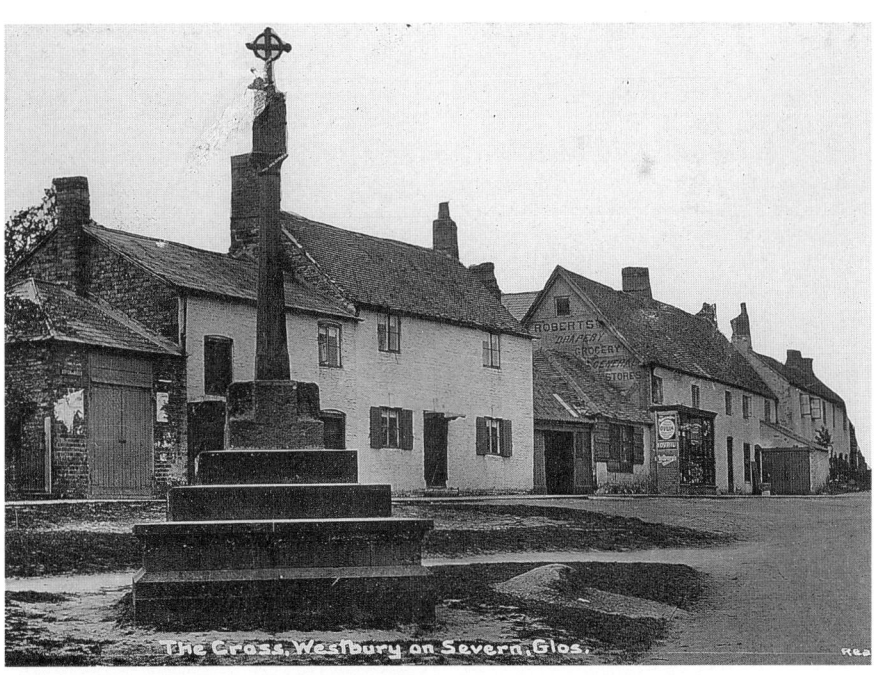

Another, earlier, view of the cross, taken about 1905.

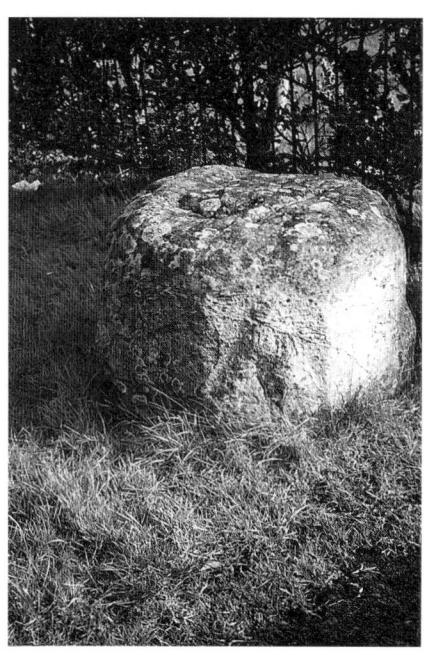

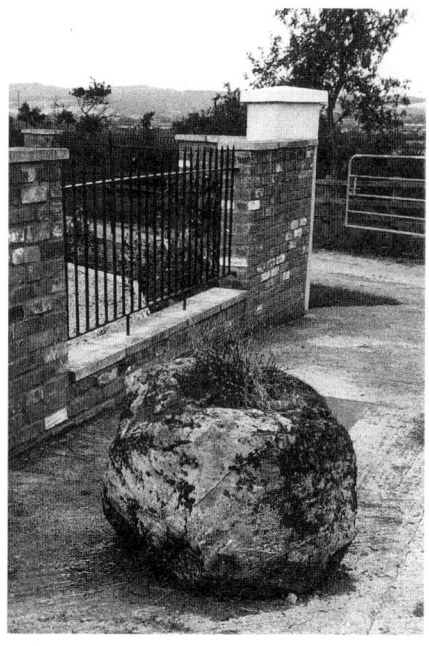

Base at Six Bells.　　　　　　　　*Base at Chaxhill (private grounds).*

WESTBURY ON SEVERN. Glos.
Chaxhill House.
NGR SO 741145 app. Sheet 162
This base now stands (1993) at the side of
the farmyard having been moved there from
the garden a few years ago. It is on private
property. It now appears roughly circular
although probably originally octagonal as
that at Six Bells. Height 25ins; 18ins across
the top with a socket-hole 13ins square,
which when seen, was filled with plants.
According to Pooley there were many others
and that they used to mark the tythings, 'of
which there are no less than thirteen in this
large parish.' (p.l).Also recorded as being
at Chaxhill House, was the statue of Charles
II which once formed part of the ancient
Wheat Market Hall which stood at the
Cross, Gloucester, but was taken down in
1749. This statue has now been set up in
Three Cocks Lane, Gloucester.

*Statue of Charles II now in Three Cocks
Lane, Gloucester.*

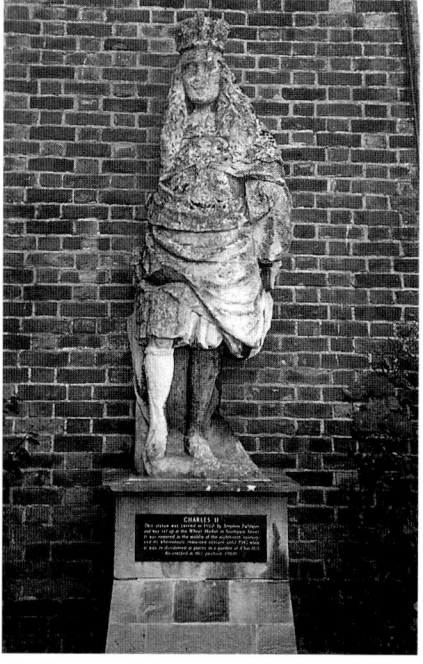

WHITCHURCH. Herefs.

NGR SO 556175 Sheet 162

The ancient church of St Dubricius is situated close to the river Wye and is renowned for its Tulip Tree in the churchyard, which, unfortunately, was practically over when we were there. The cross, which stands on four steps, is on the south side and is unusual in that both steps and socket-stone are circular. The latter measures 3ft 4ins by 2ft 2ins high, reducing in diameter halfway up by a bevel. The niche has projecting sides and pointed hood. The date, 1698, is cut into the stone. The shaft, square to octagon, has dog-tooth ornament up the angles. Both shaft and head are modern.

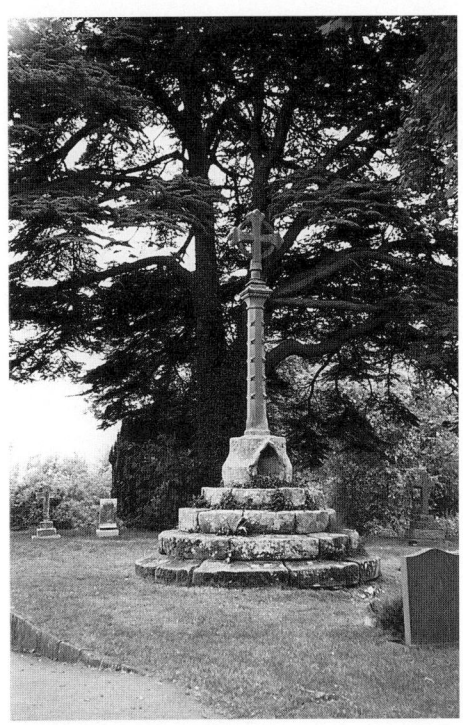

Left. *The churchyard cross.*

Below. *The church of St. Dubricius, taken from a 1930s postcard.*

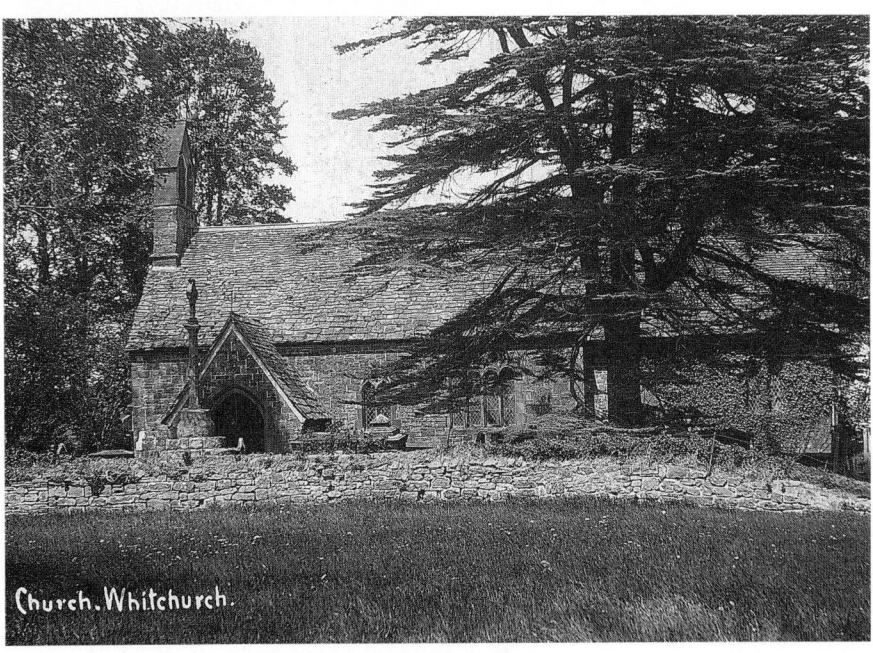

Church. Whitchurch.

WOOLASTON. Glos.
NGR SO 587993 Sheet 162
Gable Cross - in church.
On a window ledge in the north wall of the nave is a gable cross bearing the figure of Our Lord on the Cross. A notice beside it reads: 'This Crucifix is the work of medieval craftsmen, and is believed to be over 500 years old. It was removed from the apex of the church roof in 1952 for preservation.'

Churchyard.
The remains of a cross stands near the south door in Woolaston churchyard. The surface of the base stone is very pitted and worn. It appears to stand on two steps made up of small stones, but the lower one is very overgrown. The base is 32ins square and octagonal in the upper bed, brought to a square by 5ins deep broaches at the angles. It is 16ins deep. There is about 3ft of shaft remaining, octagonal to square at the bottom with stop chamfered angles, which is cemented into the base.

It often pays to walk around the outside of a church to see if any unusual stones have been used in its construction. Woolaston is a point in question, for on the outside of the north wall of the nave can be seen a cross slab with a floriate cross within a circle, used as a building stone.

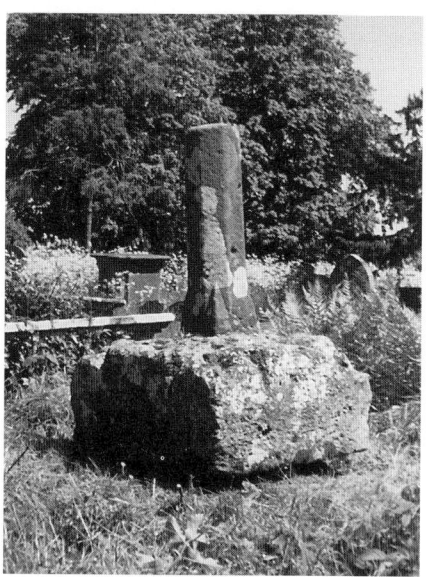

The remains of the churchyard cross.

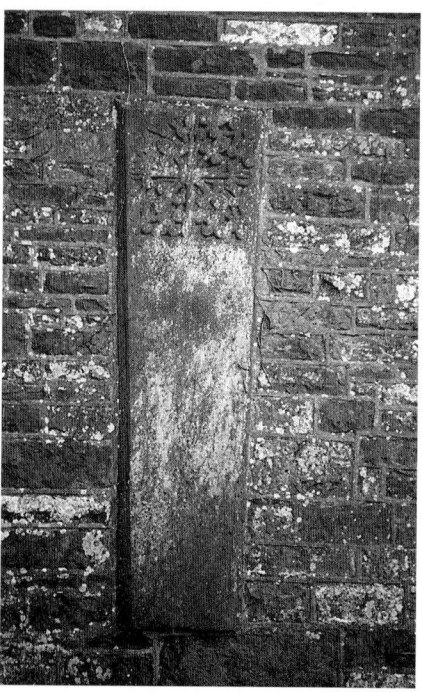

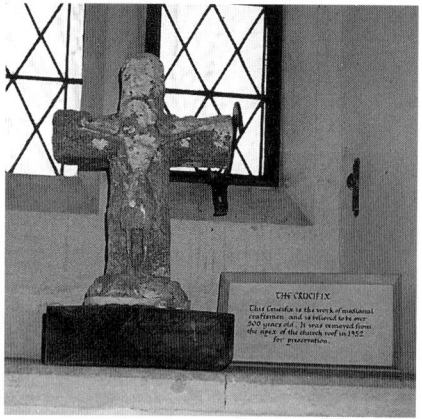

Gable cross inside the church.

Cross-slab built into outside of north wall.